You. Me.

And All That We Are

Unveiling Your Life's Beauty and Magic

A Mother's Heartfelt Testimony to Her Son

Emma Rowena

Paperback ISBN: #978-82-693637-0-8
Electronic ISBN: #978-82-693637-2-2
Audio ISBN: #978-82-693637-1-5

Photo: Pål C. Hansen. www.palhansen.com
Publishing Consultant: PRESStinely, PRESStinely.com
Published and distributed by: Golden Peacock AS

Portions of this book are works of nonfiction. Certain names and identifying characteristics have been changed.

Printed in the United States of America.

Emma Rowena Hansen
www.EmmaRowena.no

Disclaimer
The author of this book does not dispense medical advice or prescribe the use of any technique as a treatment for physical, emotional, or medical problems without the advice of a physician, either directly or indirectly. The author only intends to offer general information to help you in your quest for emotional and spiritual well-being. In the event you use any of the information in this book, the author and the publisher assume no responsibility for your actions.

To Fredrik

*And to all the sons, daughters, mothers, fathers, and carers
seeking answers to who they are
and why they're here.*

Only you hold the answers to your truth.
Only you know the love in your heart,
the beauty of your soul,
and the magnitude of your dreams.

I can only remind you,
inspire you,
love you.

Preface

You're holding in your hands a letter. It's a compilation of journal entries and revelations for my son to read when he comes of age and is ready to explore his truth and connect to his purpose in life. It's also, however, a letter to you, whether you're looking to heal from traumas of the past, seeking to discover your unique purpose, or hoping to find guidance for your journey towards a better life.

Some years ago, I discovered there was more to me and my life than I had imagined. By seeking guidance, gradually I uncovered how I was part of something bigger than the limited existence I was living. I learnt to embrace who I am, body, mind, and soul. I found ways to heal my fear, pain, and chaos, and rise to a life of empowerment, compassion, and joy.

My healing journey started the moment I knew I was pregnant. I felt my son's presence as a strong, guiding light and was inspired to find my own. We named him Fredrik, "Peaceful Ruler." It's a good name for him.

After my initial years as a mother, something in me nudged me to sign up for a healing course. It was the starting point of my path to uncover my true potential and awaken abilities in me I'd never imagined I could possess. I became a "seer" and healer. A guide. I began receiving clients, people who were on a quest to heal and discover their purpose. I guided seekers of a better life to rediscover the beauty of their unique soul and heart. Through this work, I realized how connected we all are and how the lessons I've learnt and the tools I've applied to help my clients might be valuable to other people as well. Most importantly, through Fredrik, I understood the value of guiding the younger generation to discover their true worth, strength, and beauty. I started writing this book, and it became apparent how important connecting to Fredrik's beautiful soul had been for my awakening journey.

My son is one of many young seekers today, and I'm one of many parents looking not only to live better lives but also to be wiser carers. When we as parents dare to look at our pain and fear and find ways to embrace who we are and heal, we become strong, shining guides for our children. This is the reason my book is a letter not only to Fredrik but to his peers and their parents, too.

Sometimes I direct my words to Fredrik, as I share stories that relate to him. They carry value for other readers too—young and old. Sometimes my words speak to all readers—to you— and will also be of value to Fredrik. We are indeed connected. We are all Love.

I share my story with infinite love and blessings. It's a testimony to the changes I've made in the past and how I've made my way through challenges—bearing witness to the healing they promote even as I write. Because while I share my experiences and the wisdom I've accumulated, I continue to live my life every day as a human being. Obstacles won't disappear because we've "seen the light," but as we learn to be better, brighter, more enlightened beings, we meet them with courage, strength, and wisdom. We learn to embrace and support ourselves until we find the one thing that brings us out of the dark onto our illuminated healing path again, and we remember who we are: eternal, radiant souls in a finite, physical experience.

We cannot avoid friction, but we can learn to lift our gaze and dance with it. This is what I offer to you with my story— along with a handful of tools, meditations, and exercises you can try for your own healing. Every person can apply the wisdom and knowledge I impart in this book to their lives. I hope it touches you and gives you the guidance you're seeking—and I hope you enjoy it.

Emma

Table of Contents

Preface v

Introduction ix

PART I – MASTER YOURSELF 1

Meditation – Feel the Magic 18
Exercise – Shift from Guilt to Gratitude 22
Exercise – Lean into Your Creation 23
Meditation – Lean into Your Creation 24
Meditation – Listen to Your Soul – I 27
Exercise – Shift Your Focus 31
Meditation – Shift Your Focus 32
Meditation – Listen to Your Soul – II 34
Exercise – Release Tension 37
Meditation – Shake off Disturbances 39
Exercise – Shift Water 40
Body and Soul – A Reflection 43
Meditation – Take Three Breaths 47

PART II – MASTER YOUR LIFE 51

Meditation – Discover What You Want 64
Meditation – See Yourself with the Eye of the Divine 69
The Silk Scarf – An Analogy 78
Exercise – Loosen the Knot – I 81
Exercise – Loosen the Knot – II 84
Meditation – Lean into Your Higher Self 88
Meditation – Heal Yourself 89
Exercise – "See" Your Energy Field 93

Exercise – "See" Energy Fields Around You 94
Meditation – Discover Your Truth 96
Exercise – Embrace Your Whole Self 107
Meditation – Connect Above and Below 111
Meditation – Allow the Healing 127
Exercise – Allow the Healing 129

PART III – MASTER TRANSFORMATION 131

Meditation – Love Your Body 141
Meditation – Breathe Love 143
Meditation – Reconnect to Your Essence 147

EPILOGUE 155

Acknowledgments 161

Bibliography 167

Note to Reader:

For a deeper experience of the wisdom and healing available through this book, you can access the exercise PDFs and extended audio versions of the meditations by using this QR code or by visiting www.emmarowena.no/the-book#book-resources.

Introduction

Dear Fredrik,

    Ever since before you were born, you've been teaching me about life. You've taught me to love. You've taught me about connection and how to listen and laugh. You've shown me how an embrace can be the best way out of an argument and how going your own way is possible even when you're young. You've taught me to stop and be present when you needed me to hold you and motivated me to keep searching for the best, warmest, and strongest qualities in myself. You've inspired me not only to be a better human being but to be the best mother I can be and shown me there's always an explanation for a person's choices and behaviour. Finally, you've shown me how to appreciate that love is part of my life. Always. It's part of who I am. Who we all are. Who you are.

    My love for you has no end. My admiration and faith in your integrity and your ability to make choices that ring true to your inner being are unbreakable. I'm certain you will live a rich and powerful life. You already do. I know you will listen not only to yourself but also to the people you meet along the way. You will let your light and your soul show you the right thing to do. Your light is radiant. It glows. Your talents are vast. They remain available to you as long as you let your curiosity and enthusiasm guide you and you continue exploring and playing. The beauty, my dearest, is that you value your talents and gifts without forcing them on others, and without for one second believing them to be of greater value than those of the next person. For all this, I love you. Most of all, I love you because you are.

You're about to embark on a new chapter in your young life. I've guided you as best I could from the moment I realised you had entered my life. Our connection was strong already when you were in my womb, and I remember whispering to you, "We got this, my love. Together. I'm with you every step of the way until you're ready to explore the world by yourself." Since you were born, I've communicated and shared, through words, music, and emotions, what I've felt to be true. Sometimes my guidance has been confusing, I know. I'd built my foundation on fear, rejection, and belief systems that weren't mine. When we make our way through our lives, all we can do is navigate with what we know in the moment and what we've learnt. I don't question for a second the impact your stepping into my life has had on my unfolding story—as a mother, as a human being, and as a soul.

You and I have explored our landscape together with love, light, strength, and a wisdom I never thought would be available to me. You've taught me many things and motivated me by being who you are, yes, but I've also found wisdom in myself by accepting the roles of mother and teacher.

It's as if the resonance of my soul, once hidden deep in my heart, found a timbre in your presence—like the vibration of a song or an instrument—that made my soul ring stronger and clearer, until I could recognise it and reconnect to who I am. I believe the vibration of my soul has confirmed and rejuvenated your unique timbre too, as I learnt, grew, and healed.

Today I sit here at the kitchen table in our little home by the Oslo fjord, surrounded by our wild garden with the big oak tree and a view of the sea and the forest, and with classical music streaming from the radio—a fresh cup of oat latte in front of me. We moved here a few years ago after our lives had taken an unexpected turn. It's not a grand place—it's what we could manage—our cosy home.

Sometimes the challenge of living in this old house has overwhelmed me, with the leaking pipes, cold floors, and the mice seeking refuge in our ceiling. Still, it's peaceful— and at times, magical. Never have I heard such intense, vibrant birdsong, and never have I felt the moon and the stars so strongly. Your school is just minutes away, there's always been room for your friends to stop by, and I love having been able to work from home as much as I have. That way, I could be here for you, embrace you, and guide you when you needed me to as I watched you develop into the fine young man you're becoming. We've spent countless beautiful moments here, many times only you and me, but often with friends and family. I'm deeply grateful for our time together in this lush little place.

Soon we must leave this home, however. Our lives are taking another turn, and fresh adventures await. It's not an unexpected change, although it's sooner than I'd hoped. It's how it is. Nothing ever stays the same (nor should it). We move and learn. Sometimes we stumble and fall, but if we dare to listen to the wisdom of our souls, we grow, heal, and rise to our fullest potential as human beings, with our radiant souls as unrelenting guides.

I'm ready to show you what I've discovered on my journey thus far. You are part of this adventure because, although it started before you came into the world, the path only opened after I'd come to know you. This is the tale of your mother and her healing, enlightening exploration. But it's also a story about you, and all you can choose to live and be. It holds the essence of all I've learnt and experienced as I've watched you grow.

Your soul knows the teachings I'm about to offer, though you might have forgotten. When you were a little boy, you shared a multitude of visions and experiences with me: deep wisdom and elevated truths. You shut them out at some point, and when I asked, "Aren't you curious about what more is 'out there?", you answered, with the quirky clarity that never ceases to baffle and amuse me, "Why should I spend my life trying to be in a place that I'm going to after I'm done with this life, anyway? I'd rather enjoy being here while I can." Why should you…

No one can express such profound insights better than you, but what if you can enjoy this life with the beauty and magic of that "place" as part of it? What if bringing the greater picture into your presence here on earth can brighten your life and bring you strength, clarity, and peace? What if we can live our lives as an expression of all that we are— human, soul, light, and love? We can, you know. We can make it amazing. Not only that; we can help other people lift their gaze too and show them their beauty and their possibilities. That's how we can change our world.…

In this journal—this letter to you—I want to show you how we can embrace these possibilities. My desire to write it all down started a while ago, growing like a pregnancy, like you did before you came into the world. As is true for every child, your first steps were without direction, containing only one aim: to walk. One step at a time. Yet they held the promise of all you could be. They were your first steps on the long trail that's been unfolding as you move through your life. This book started in much the same way, with a few words whose only purpose was to write. One word at a time. The direction revealed itself as I wrote, and in the end, it's become my gift to you for your journey onwards. As I sat at our kitchen table, and sometimes in my studio in the garden, or on the ferry that takes me into the city, the words revealed themselves. They are my humble testimony to you.

You're free to do with this letter as you wish, of course. Take what you want from it whenever you like. Listen to your own voice, and then seek my guidance if it feels right. Explore my words when your curiosity gets the better of you. I trust you will discard what doesn't resonate with you. That's why I dare write this to you. You're standing in your own power now, and all I can do is offer my perspective. You will find yours. Of this, I have no doubt.

Emma Rowena Hansen

My dearest Fredrik, I welcome you to your continuing journey. I hope what I have to share can give you guidance and show you how to live your life from joy, curiosity, and strength—especially through the challenges and moments of confusion that will come your way.

Enjoy.

Explore.

Embrace the journey the way only you can.

PART I
MASTER YOURSELF

Somewhere along the line, a voice advised me to write a book. It was like a whisper from my soul. One day, I sat down and started, and here I am, writing a book of inspiration to my son, Fredrik, as he embarks on his life as a young adult. His journey is bound to offer both challenges and joy, and my aim is to show him how to meet those challenges with strength, confidence, kindness, and curiosity. I pray he will embody joy with gratitude, ease, and grace.

My name is Emma. I'm Norwegian, British, and a citizen of the world. I'm a woman, a mother, a child, a crone. I'm a friend, a lover, a daughter, sister, aunt, and godmother. I'm feminine and masculine, tall, slender, ginger-haired, with grey-green eyes, and freckles. I'm attractive at times—and a wreck at others. Sometimes I talk a lot, and sometimes I'm silent. I move, expand, learn, and teach. I stumble and I rise. My overworking mind worries me when there is nothing to worry about. My experiences have influenced my life's journey and defined who I've become: a musician, healer, and "seer." I'm a lover of music, good food, birdsong, trees, the sea, the sun, my beautiful dog… and, of course, my son—this amazing young man who keeps stimulating me to see better, listen better, and do better. He's tall, handsome, and clever. His light astounds people, and some people feel he belongs to another time. To me, he belongs to all ages—the past and the future—as he carries both the manners of a past time and the intellectual capacity and clear visions of the future. Most of all, he belongs to our age today, as he carries a wisdom and awareness that our world is calling for. There's a reason he's here. There's a reason all the young people of today are here. They hold the strength to move our world to a better place.

My journey has been demanding, and there have been times when I've lost myself in the turmoil of life. My biggest strength, perhaps, is that I've never stopped. I've never given up. I've spent the last few years seeking to recover my essence: my core. I've found it, lost it, regained it. I still lose it at times, until I remember who I am once more. I'm imperfect and perfect, broken and whole, hollow and full. I'm doubtful and fearful, but more and more, I have faith, and I trust. I believe—nay, I *know* there's more to the world than we can fathom with our rational minds. Finally, I can hear my voice. I'm ready to take my chances and reveal who I am through words, music, and presence. I'm a soul, a spirit, energy, power, and emotion. I'm love. I'm human.

So, what story have I let define me? How and from what perspective have I created my world? Where has it taken me? And why should you care? Well… let's go back. Let's go back almost to the beginning.…

I've spent the greater part of my life in agony and fear. Yup. It's true. Even as a child, I let fear govern my world. Where did that fear come from? Let me rephrase: where did the *feeling* of fear come from? I could ramble on about my childhood now. I won't. There's nothing unique about my childhood. I experienced love, rejection, joy, trauma, good relations, and poor relations. Thousands of authors have written about the pain of childhood and its influence on life. Their books might shed light on our choices and emotions and might help us choose a different path, but what I'm curious about now is the hidden beliefs (which may or may not have come from my childhood) that led me to put fear in charge of my life.

Until recently, fear was my default. I wasn't aware of it—it was a state of being. I didn't recognise it as fear. It permeated my every movement, emotion, thought, and belief. Was it the sensation of being of no consequence that nourished my fear?

Was it the devastating experience of being worthless? Or was it the other way around? What came first? Whatever the case, fear and lack of worth have held hands with me throughout my life. They became my best friends and my worst enemies, but also (as time revealed) my best teachers.

I've been fearful in most areas of my life, but particularly when there was something I wanted to accomplish, like playing the piano. Inspired by my music-loving, piano-playing father, I used my gift of music, applied my natural talent, and worked hard to become a pianist. It was a constant struggle. Whether I was accompanying outstanding performers on stage or practicing in my little studio, Ms Fear and her friend, Ms Unworthy, were present.

Because I felt I was of little value, performing and playing the piano became the one area in which I thought I could prove myself to be something other than an inadequate human being who didn't fit in. Indeed, part of my fear was that I couldn't fit in. Ever. When you don't fit in, what could be better than standing out? And what better place to stand out than on a stage—stepping out from the masses (believing that they have excluded you, anyway) and rising above them?

The trouble is, when you play piano from fear, you lose sight (let's face it) of the whole point: the music! Walking onto a stage puts you in the spotlight for scrutiny, exposing every mistake and illuminating any lack of talent. Being "perfect" becomes the only solution. Or so it seems. However, perfect is impossible. There are too many people and too many variables in this world for anyone to label any form of being human more perfect than anything else. The Japanese have a different perception of "perfection" than, say, the Nigerians, Brits, Peruvians, Cubans, or Norwegians. For example, Cubans see the "skinny" ideal women in the Western world strive to attain as unhealthy and "sick" (I agree!), whereas Cuban women prefer to be curvy and voluptuous. Within any culture, you'll find countless views on perfection. There must be as many ideals of perfection as there are people.

As I couldn't find a way to "fit in" with any group, I thought perfection on stage was the solution. Then I could be admired and feel of value. At the same time, I feared being "found out," so

I played most of the time with other soloists, hiding behind their backs. Then, when people approached me after performances to say something positive about my playing—that the music had moved them or that my playing was beautiful—I was sure they were lying. I imagined they secretly thought I was a fraud. ("Why on earth would they say anything at all?" you might ask. Well, exactly!) It was never me, I thought. It was the people I had played with who had moved them. Because I knew—and I figured they knew it too—I wasn't perfect. I was anything but: inadequate technique, countless mistakes, lack of focus and expression, and so on. My mind was brilliant at letting me in on the details of my imperfection. It was the one thing my mind managed perfectly....

Yet a voice inside me kept telling me there was something I was missing, that I was holding back my true potential—in my music, in my relationships, and in every aspect of my life. Every time someone said something to the effect of, "I'm not sure what to make of you as a pianist—whether I like what you do, or not" (which is what someone told me once), my soul said, *But that's because there's more to me than you can hear now. I know there is....*

Somewhere deep within, I knew I was holding back my potential. In bright glimpses of "seeing," I could almost believe that one day I would play my music. Music from the depths of my soul. Alone on stage, or with (or even in front of) a group of other brilliant musicians. Maybe I had something to say. Something to which people would want to listen. Maybe my music would move them. Every time I wanted to give up playing—and believe me, I tried to stop several times— something kept me going. I told people I was quitting, and the next minute that I was going to create music… talk about laying a trap for myself.

But guess what? Now I'm playing my music. Alone. Me and my piano. What's more, I'm enjoying it. I do have something to contribute. Even with my voice—this voice I never dared use from the moment I started studying music. I couldn't and wouldn't sing. Accompanying all those amazing singers didn't help—while my respect for the art of the voice grew, it only enhanced my sense of shortcoming as a singer. I convinced myself I was a fraud at the instrument I was supposed to specialise in—so how could I imagine I might have something to say with my voice?

I closed my mouth and stopped singing. For years, I didn't even hum in the shower. In my early childhood, I shut down my natural expression, and hiding my voice was a step in the same direction. Little by little, I became convinced I didn't know how to do anything. As part of my story, I cultivated the belief that I didn't have the codes we need to function and succeed as human beings. I convinced myself I'd failed socially, artistically, and intellectually, in my appearance, my actions, in love, in my humour, in my everything.

People who have met me over the years—especially once I got past those humbling and frightening teens—might not see how this could be possible. I became an expert at hiding my true self—my emotions, thoughts, ideas, and my passion. I believed I was of no value and did everything I could to disguise any weakness. What remained was a clever, well-behaved girl with good posture (sometimes even well-dressed, if not "trendy" or good-looking). Beneath the mask was confusion, anger, and resentment. That was it. No love. No passion. No genuine joy. I never, ever had a sense of peace or contentment. I was on guard. I was self-centred in my fear of being found out and was always on the lookout for the "right way." Every moment, I had a watchful eye on "the others." Could they see through my façade of "being someone"?

It was exhausting. When I look back now (and it hasn't been that long), I can't believe I kept myself going. How could I think this performance could work, be good, or even make sense? More incomprehensible still is that I assumed hiding my own passions could lead me to a better place. There was always a longing for a better place….

Looking back now, I see I had no connection to my sense of self—to my emotions, intuition, power, self-love, worthiness… or to the love of others. I had no connection to my essence, my truth. I kept churning, trying to decipher the rules, codes, and stories that flourish "out there." "The others" seemed to get something I didn't. They seemed to fit in somewhere. The trouble was they all fit in differently according to who and where they were, and I had to keep shifting and changing my personality to fit in with them. I thought everyone had the knowledge required to live, love, and flourish. Everyone but me. Ha! Was I mistaken. I see it now, thank goodness.

Having swum through the muddy waters of my self-doubt and stepped onto the shore on the other side, I see how others—those people I used to copy and look up to—struggled in their own type of mud. They all—almost, for there are exceptions—wrestled with their own sense of not "getting it." Some found their way to shore. Some are still treading water.

I'm lucky—I'm stubborn. A voice in me wouldn't stop nudging me, telling me not to stop, insisting that one day I would play my music with joy. I would perform the music my way, with my own genuine expression. People would listen. They would want to hear what I have to say and the stories I have to tell. I would inspire them to find their own inner voice and start telling their stories, too.

That inner voice is the voice that urged me to write this book. I hope it will move you, touch you. I hope to encourage you to be as stubborn as I am and not give up until you get some answers. Your answers.

I started this book the same way I started creating my music: first one word, one sentence, one paragraph, then several pages. Through my journey of rediscovering myself and tuning in to my inner voice, I've learnt to trust and follow what comes to mind. The inner voice, the voice of my soul (or higher self, inner self, intuition, or God—whatever it may be) brings forth discoveries and experiences, enabling my mind to convey them in whichever way I decide. Such as through music. Or words. My mind is full of unnecessary and disturbing thoughts, but it's also curious and open. I've let fear constrain me, but when I let my soul guide my mind (and not the other way around), my mind can investigate experiences with curiosity and trust, and I can receive what comes. I can listen and follow the guidance—whether it be from my inner voice or a higher wisdom.

With that awareness, I sat down and asked the nudging voice—my soul—what to do. I was determined not to let the old notion of "the others get it; I don't" stop me. What did the voice say? It told me to write. To begin with a word. Then a sentence. And then…

So here we are. Hello, by the way. I value your being here. I hope you're ready to explore and see where the words take us. I am. I have an intense sense of excitement and impatience in me. I have a lot to say. I wonder if I can find the right words….

Minutes later, back at the kitchen table—this time with a fresh cup of tea…

There. I'm back. I had to make myself a hot drink, as the impatience was getting the better of me. Now I'm sitting here with my delicious peppermint tea, ready to allow the words to flow once more.

Out the window, I see my favourite view. Our old, majestic oak tree's bare branches reach up towards the light blue winter sky. The ground is white with fresh snow. I love that tree. It stands there, going about its business—being strong. Peaceful. Not minding the cold, not questioning anything. They say oak trees spend 500 years growing, and another 500 years dying. This tree is still growing. Its trunk is thickening, its crown expanding. When I look at it, it inspires me to be strong. It reminds me to go about my life in my way. It reminds me to keep growing….

Where were we? Ah, yes. To fear or not to fear.

I've told you I'm a pianist who thought nothing of herself most of her life, but who stepped out of the dark and saw herself—and valued her own expression. I've drawn the words "soul," "magic," "intuition," and "energy" into my vocabulary. I've opened to new realities. It took time, though. I'll try to explain, but please remember, everything I share is my perception and experience. It's not the only truth….

First, there's the culture I live in: Norway—the land of fjords, beautiful nature, northern lights, and wealth. It's the land of smoked salmon, brown cheese, and wild berries. The land of Henrik Ibsen, Edvard Grieg, and A-ha—our first world-famous pop band. It's the land of the Nobel Peace Prize, the Oslo Deal, and of a very popular king, King Harald V. Why is he popular? Because he represents the best of what we are—

or of what we want to be. He's a fair, just, and kind king—private, but with compassion for his people, and a lovely sense of humour. He represents tradition, and he's tuned in to the shifts of time, supporting people in need and welcoming his children's controversial life partners—partners "from the people" rather than from the European aristocracy—into his family with warmth and generosity. We call him—as we did his father—"the people's king." He balances the contrast between his royal privileges and the social-democratic ideas of equal economic allocation that governs our country in the best possible way, so his people—royalists or not—all appreciate and love him. You might say he's the king of a "socialist kingdom."

Apart from the centuries the Danes and Swedes governed our country, Norway is an old kingdom. It's the kingdom of the Vikings, of cross-country skiing, and of the trolls. Today, people here say trolls are only fairy tales. Alongside the "little people" that were once an integrated and natural part of Norwegians' daily lives, they've all been assigned to fantasy and superstition. They no longer have anything to do with reality. In our beautiful country, full of privileged people, "reality" has become the new religion. ("What is reality, though?" I ask. Let's see, shall we?)

Living in a social democratic country, we try to believe fairness can be a guiding principle in the world (we don't always agree on how, of course). We like to think we're a peaceful and just people—like our king—and in most ways we are. However, these days, Norwegians live for the most part in the material world. (Again, this is my observation. Yours might be different.) With the magic and myths that were a natural part of our ancestors' lives lost, our biggest political debates today circle around varying degrees of freedom, control, fear of strangers, and economic and gender equality (the latter sometimes seeping into the intimate parts of our relationships: the man must not be too masculine, and the woman not too feminine…). Our official religion is Lutheran Christianity (no room for angels there). Our unofficial religion is the amazing wealth gained from North Sea oil. It's a lottery ticket that causes quite the identity crisis in these times of climate distress: we want the oil to stop polluting our world, yet we're not ready to give up the material and financial privileges the oil brings. Being Norwegian is not as easy as it may appear....

Norwegians are shy, subdued, and reserved, and (like the British, my other heritage) not accustomed to displaying their emotions. They're friendly, loyal, and eager to help in a crisis but terrified of small talk, flirtation, and blatant displays of celebration. I heard a man from an African country speak of Norway as the "underdeveloped country of 'life joy.'" He believed that, in our attempt to handle the harsh realities of life, we've forgotten how to enjoy ourselves. Laughter, dance, and play are not natural parts of our days, and people dismiss words like "soul" and "energies" as "superstitious," "airy," or "New Agey" (which, to some people, are all the same thing). The typical Norwegian has put the idea of there being a greater picture and more to life than meets the eye in a casket and sealed it shut. If you try to convince them fairies and angels exist, they'll look at you like you're crazy. Or worse, they'll pity you for being naïve and gullible. It's no wonder those who long to reconnect to the beauty of the unseen (the spiritual realm) keep their quest hidden (as I once did). Magic has left the stage, and in its stead, wealth and the rational mind have entered. For now. There's one beautiful exception to this picture: Mother Nature. Her magic still captures Norwegians, and on any sunny holiday, you'll find our mountain paths and forests brimming with people (many of whom are, I imagine, indulging in the secret desire to discover the forgotten wonders).

In this subdued, sober social democratic environment, stepping out of the crowd to share my new experience of the sky and beyond—soul, magic, angels, and all—meant risking being ridiculed and expelled from my crowd and from society, and even from my family and the world as I knew it. It was daunting. I was terrified, especially because I'd spent my whole life doing everything in my power to fit in. It took a long time before I dared reveal to people how my new reality differed from the "truths" my culture insisted upon. I'd never accepted them fully, though. (How could I? I was too busy being afraid.) I'd always kept a secret door open to the mysterious "unseen." Which is the reason I discovered it, I suppose.

I had more reasons for hiding. First, I've always shied away when people tried to force their experiences and realities upon me. Second, I wanted to tread gently and allow people to discover "the new me" themselves. However, people often don't "get" or accept "the new you," no matter how you break it to them. Either they pull away or they heap ridicule on you. Or—and this is the beautiful and interesting part—they tap into the new you, draw inspiration from your transformation, and start on their own healing path. You lose some, you face some obstacles, and you win some. I assure you, if you choose to investigate a new reality, you'll encounter other souls on a similar journey, and you'll make new friends along the way. It happened to me.

The third reason for hiding my new discoveries was my reluctance to take on the label "New Age." Yes, my experiences and revelations these past few years have taken me to mind-blowing places and given me a so-called "New Age" perspective on life, but there's more to it than that. Life in its entirety—magic, glory, and all—is more than a label. Any label on any belief system, whether we embrace the system or shy away from it, is only that: a label. Every belief system human beings have held throughout time has relied upon a structure of strange (albeit interesting) systems, rules, and patterns, as well as rhythms. All of them have formed as we sought to discover the essence of who we are. Ah, yes, we humans have always been searching for the truth.

However, we don't need these frameworks to discover our truth. In fact, they might distract us from it. (The frameworks can be a comforting guiding force, I get it. There's beauty in that, too.) Instead, we can investigate and listen. And trust. Trust that there's more to life than what we perceive with our physical senses. Trust that there is love, peace, and a Higher Truth. Trust that we carry the key to a Higher Wisdom. Every one of us.

So simple… yet so hard to discover.

I can't judge anyone for the way they express themselves, although I might not always agree with them or like their expressions. Every word written and every revelation shared by any one person will be valuable to someone—for inspiration, as a lesson, or as a guiding principle. I only want you to remember this: anything anyone (including me) tells you is part of their story and stems from their personal journey. Their guidance can serve as a tool for you on your journey, a reminder of who you are (or of who you're not—which is a valuable awareness too), but it can never be your whole truth. No one can possess the whole truth, and certainly not someone else's truth. We're human, and our humanness will always limit our perspective regardless of how long we meditate or search.

It's time to confess: I'm a "New Age and Life Philosophy Consumer." Yup. It's true. For some time now, I've been buying help and services in the alternative wellness field whenever I found I was stuck. The lessons I've learnt have been vital for my healing journey, but they never showed me the entire picture. They never revealed the one-and-only answer. I've had life-changing revelations, and I've touched upon what I've perceived to be pure truth. The most potent lesson has been this: my truth stems from my search and my inner wisdom, my soul. Not from another person's life story or from a structure with a label. In my experience, labels and structures diminish the truth and beauty of all that we are, all that we come from, and all that we can be.

Now, as I write, I'll share experiences that come to me regardless of which dimension, realm, or belief system they might relate to. I'm human and I'm more than human, and I will share what I've discovered—from my perspective. I can never give you the one-and-only answer, but maybe I can inspire you to search and listen to your own wisdom. Maybe what I have to say will strike a chord in you and entice you to investigate within yourself. You choose what to believe, and how you wish to read my words. I claim only this: we all have a soul—a subtle, intangible part we cannot measure, see, or touch but that we sense nevertheless. Like a whisper. Our soul is part of us, though it's easy to dismiss, as there's no measurable way to prove its existence. We must notice it within ourselves. Essentially, my soul is what I am, and my physical being is an earthly manifestation of it. My soul permeates every cell in my physical body. It influences every action I take and every reflection I have, because I *am* my soul.

I'm also, at times, separated from the voice of my soul. Growing up in a "civilised" society, I learnt to be rational and "think" my way through life—until I forgot who I am. When the pain of not knowing who I am became too great to bear, I started searching. That's when I reconnected. The beauty I discovered is that because I am me, a soul, I cannot lose myself. My soul is always here, even in my darkest moments. *I* am always here. As are you. You are an eternal soul. You cannot fall apart, no matter how or where you express yourself. You are always you. A soul. Can you grasp it?

Decades ago, a few men of authority (Sigmund Freud and Carl Jung are perhaps the most famous) claimed to have found an explanation for the invisible aspects of human life. They called it our "subconscious," and it became a truth people all over the world accepted. Today, we use the word "subconscious" without hesitation. It's become part of our general knowledge (at least in the Western world). Yet none of us get what the subconscious *is*. Carl Jung stated that as there's a limit to what our conscious mind can hold, we need an additional storehouse for our "hidden" knowledge and prior experience. Jung and Freud called this storehouse and the knowledge stored there the subconscious. There's more to the term, I understand, but to me, it still makes more sense to talk about having a soul, an aspect greater than our conscious mind that knows and sees all, including what our consciousness perceives. Our physical form and the noise surrounding us might restrain and disturb our souls, but we can perceive our souls the moment we pause and tune in to their voices. The soul peeks through whenever we let it. It whispers guidance in our ears. It pushes us forward when we need it.

We live in a time in which people are searching for reconnection. We want to be more than a mind with extra storage. We no longer trust an old authority. We want to come home to our own truth, rediscover who we are, and get to know our souls. We want to heal, thrive, and shine. It's who we are.

Believing we have a soul isn't new, of course. Human beings have spoken of it and acknowledged it for centuries, though during the "enlightened age," when our minds became our leading stars, we expressed our souls for the main part in worship and religious devotion. For the rest of the time, we might have replaced the term, we might have added different packaging to it, and we might even have pretended it wasn't there. But no matter what you believe and where you are, your soul has always been with you, and it's there to stay. It won't let you down or let you off the hook. It will keep reminding you of its existence until you're ready to hear it, receive it, and embrace it. New Age, you say? It's okay. It can still be true and valuable—if we listen to the core of the message.

I mentioned earlier another "New Age" term: *We are connected.* Can you comprehend it? Let's explore. Think of a friend or someone in your family. Notice the feeling that follows the thought. It has a certain vibe, doesn't it? Does it make you smile? Frown? Does a colour come to mind? A song, a smell, or a physical sensation? Many people say these sensations are "just memories," but to me they also speak of connection. Try focusing on the effect of that "memory"—can you sense a "textural sensation" that belongs only to the person who is part of the memory? Shift your focus to someone else. Can you sense the difference? This reveals not only your own feelings for these people; it reveals your perception of their essence, and your connection to them.

Let's take another example. Imagine you're going to a party. You're feeling great and you can't wait to meet other people, eat good food, dance.... You meet an old friend who wants to share his story. It's a story of loss, pain, and regret. During his account, you notice you've become tired. You're ready to go home. What's wrong with you?

The following day, you find yourself in a stressful meeting. People are arguing, and the atmosphere is tense. The same tiredness hits you, and you question your health. A colleague enters with a joke and a big smile. Her spirits are high. The atmosphere in the room changes. People relax, smile, shake hands. Your tiredness is gone, and you leave the meeting optimistic. Hopeful. Do you see the picture?

Another example: You're walking home from a painful meeting with an ex. You feel lonely, sad, and angry. A stranger passes you and gives you a big, warm smile. It isn't a lot, and it's over in a second, but your sadness lifts. As if by magic. You wonder, "What was all the fuss about?" You look forward to spending the rest of the day with people you love.

We take these experiences for granted: "Of course a smile will make you feel better," and "Of course there will be tension when people disagree about something important." But there's more to it, I promise. We—our souls—emanate energy, a vibration. Our emotions hold energy, too. Consider how different anger and joy feel in your body. One is denser than the other, don't you agree? They transform your natural energy. You feel them physically.

For instance, often, we perceive anger and fear in our stomachs and jaws, grief in our chests, and joy... all over. In our toes, even. We also radiate these emotions out beyond our physical selves, and people around us pick up on them. Whether through our pure soul vibration or through our emotions, our energy affects other people.

Think about it. Do you have a friend or a colleague who drains you, causing you to feel tired every time you meet them? Do you know someone who lifts your spirits, leaving you feeling strong and joyful when you're with them? Often, we blame the other person: "It's their way of talking to me" or "It's their way of judging the way I dress." Or, on a positive note, it's "their humour" or "their kindness." Sometimes we call it "chemistry." Sometimes we blame ourselves. "There's something wrong with me." There's nothing wrong with you. You're connected, that's all. You sense people's energies. You feel high, uplifting energies when others are happy, and you feel low, depressing energies when they're in pain. Some people carry a heavier energy, as their life experience is one of pain or anger (which usually comes from being in pain). Others hold a lighter energy, as their life view is more positive, optimistic, and joyful. Our minds want to complicate it, but it's simple (if we could only listen to our hearts). You pick up on others' energies, and others pick up on yours. You feel them. They feel you. Even when you think about someone—positively or negatively—you connect to them. They might not recognise consciously that they're picking up on your vibration, but at some level, they are. Energy travels fast and far. It's powerful. Your thoughts can help others feel better. They may even cause someone to call you out of the blue. As if by magic.

Yes, magic....

I believe in magic. True magic. I never used to. I was convinced life was hard, miserable, and frightening. I didn't agree with my dad when he insisted that after death there is nothing (he knows better now, having passed over—I can sense him, bless him). But I didn't believe in magic. I didn't dare. I was lonely, consumed with fear, terrified of being different, and desperate to discover the "right" social codes. I believed I was a mistake. Magic was fantasy. It was the last thing I was ready to embrace.

But now. Ah, now... Everything is different. I not only believe in magic; I trust it. I open to it, play with it, and create with it. Most of the time.

Today, I cannot imagine a world without magic. It took a while, but as I discovered my new reality, I felt the magic around me and the magic within me. It's all about perspective. Of course it is. Ask yourself, "Do I see the magic around me? Or do I see only harshness and trouble?" Can you, just for a moment, allow yourself to be the child you once were and marvel at the butterfly's colours, the bird's song, the new leaves in spring? Can you remember the excitement? Try it. And then try rejecting the idea that there's magic in the world. You don't have to say it out loud. Explore it for yourself. Give the experience a chance. You're living proof of the magic. You made it into this world. You breathe, move, feel, create. (You do. Every word you utter and every action you take is your creative choice). You grow, learn, live, and love.

Don't take my word for it. Stop. Discover!

Meditation – Feel the Magic

Take a deep breath and focus on the statement: "There's magic all around."

Contemplate deeply—take your time. Then consider:

You.
Are.
Magic.

In and of yourself. Connected to All That Is.

Feel it in your heart. Sense it in your soul, beyond your thoughts. Investigate. Be curious, like a child. The magic emanates from Creation and seeps into your human existence. If you allow it, you will recognise it. All you need to do is wonder.

I feel the urge to have fun. I'll leave you for now and go over to my studio to play the piano. Go—listen to music. Indulge in something you love. Wonder at the beauty. That too is magic.

Dearest Fredrik,

I'm overjoyed to have you with me. Every day I feel thankful. We've had our struggles, and it hasn't been an easy ride, but we have each other. The love I hold for you is unparalleled.

It's the unconditional force of life. I'm certain you recognise it....

This morning I'm going into the city to work, and I'm sitting on the pier, waiting for the ferry. Living on this beautiful peninsula in the Oslo fjord has its perks. Commuting will never be the same after having lived in this special place. After a five-minute bus ride, we get to sit on the pier for a few minutes. Before boarding the ferry, we can watch the sunrise, listen to the seabirds, or chat with a neighbour. On the ferry we can buy a cup of coffee and a svele. Every ferry in Norway has them. They resemble American pancakes—but better—and we eat them with traditional brown cheese. Yummy. We can sit in a comfortable seat (there's always a seat) and continue to chat with a neighbour, or we can prepare for a meeting, write a paragraph for our book, or look out on the fjord in quiet contemplation. In winter we keep warm inside, and in summer when the sun is shining, we sit out on deck and take in the sea's scent and the view of the fjord with all the little islands scattered around, the land, green with trees, rising from the water, the hills in the distance, and the city of Oslo with its characteristic city hall, its shape inspired by our "national" brown cheese (would you believe it?), emerging as we approach it. In the evenings a stunning sunset sometimes colours the sea a deep orange or purple. It's a privileged life, and I feel blessed to be living in this beautiful nature with the sea close by, and my beloved Fredrik with me—at least for a few more years. (What will I do the day he leaves his nest to explore the world on his own?)

The ferry just arrived. Back in a moment!

Minutes later…

There. I found a seat by the window. I have a svele in my hand and my Mac in front of me. I'm ready to continue.…

I had so much fun writing yesterday, I found it difficult to focus at the piano. My head was drooping, and my body felt heavy. The playing made me tired. I was trying to have fun, but I wasn't *having* fun. My fear of not living up to the magic I was telling you about got the better of me. I short-circuited the flow, so to speak, by trying too hard instead of being in the moment and observing what my soul wanted to play. There was no point continuing until I let go of the trying. Were you aware that when you *try* to create—when you make an effort—you lower your energy and choke your creativity? *Being* and *doing* is the only way. Next time I'll just play.

Vibration. Energy. More "New Age" words. Are they new? Of course not. The words have been part of our vocabulary long before the New Age wave appeared on the scene. All the concepts of "New Age religion" are old. We, the people who have turned our backs on magic, the soul, and energy, are the new ones. Through our reliance on our "rational" minds, we have become detached from the greater picture. The concepts highlighted, explored, and worshipped through the New Age movement are ancient. Of course, "ancient" is also a "New Age" concept. It seems the world needed a New Age.

Energy, magic, and the soul: it's all arcane wisdom re-emerging in our world. Apart from a few wise men and women, our modern societies have lost the wisdom of the ancients—we've hidden it under a veil of rationality. However, a new age is rising. We see it in the multitude of people seeking guidance and the many people offering their newfound wisdom. The longing to reconnect is becoming too strong to ignore. Our souls are tugging at our hearts, asking us to wake up. They urge us to open up, wonder, and embrace. There are still people who seek to fill the void through destruction, but an increasing number of people are ready for a better world. A better life.

Yes, life. Birth and death and everything in between. Power. Action. Struggle. Pain. But also Joy. Excitement. Creativity. Those sexy aspects of life.

Life is an eternal journey of exploration, healing, fear, release, and love. Your life's journey can take on unprecedented dimensions if you embrace it. It can take you to a better place. (Remember? The place I was looking for but couldn't find? Once upon a time…) A better place is always a possibility. For everyone. But to find a better place, we must manage the energy we put out into the world.

Let's look closer at the topic of energy, then. That which permeates everything and which we all radiate. The mystery we're uncovering these days is how much influence we have on the *way* we radiate energy. Our energy affects not only other people but plants, trees, animals, food, and our bodies. When the Swedish retailer IKEA put two plants in a schoolyard and played a recording of insults over one and a recording of supportive compliments over the other, the first plant withered while the second one—the one showered with compliments—thrived.[1] The researchers gave the two

---

[1] *New York Post*, May 8, 2018, https://nypost.com/2018/05/08/students-insult-plants-in-unique-anti-bullying-experiment/.

plants the same amount of light, air, and water. Only the messages in the recordings ("You look rotten," "Are you even alive?" versus "I like you the way you are," "You're making a difference in the world") were different.

Given this, can you imagine the impact your thoughts have on your body when you eat? Consider this: if you eat something with the words, "I shouldn't. It's bad for me," what are you instilling in the food and, through the food, into your body? The body not only has to digest the food but the negative emotions, as well. The type of emotions that cause a plant to wither and die.

We're so full of shame and guilt in our world today, it's a wonder we can bear it. Here's a challenge for you:

Exercise – Shift from Guilt to Gratitude

For the rest of the day, try changing any guilty, shameful, or fearful thoughts into loving, excited, thankful ones with every bite of food you eat and every sip of liquid you drink. As you bring a glass of water to your mouth, say to yourself "Ah… What a clear, refreshing drink!" Or, with your coffee, say, "Mmmm. I love this flavour." With your dinner, say, "This food is amazing," and with your bite of chocolate, "M-m-m, what a delicious treat."

I know it might seem crazy and fake at first, but you have nothing to lose, right? All I'm asking is that you try it, observe, and notice how it feels. It might even change what you eat, as you're enjoying giving your body great experiences.

Mmmm. I just took a bite of my svele—a treat often labelled "not good for you." I delighted in its flavour, discovering the sensations on my tongue and in my mouth. Being curious elevates your thoughts and shifts your focus. When you focus on exploring the sensations from what you eat, there is no room for shame or guilt. It feels great, and anything that feels great adds higher, elevating vibrations—and emotions—to your body. It's a gift.

I must pause and tell you how thrilled I am to be chatting away with you like this: allowing all topics great and small to show up. It's like being a sculptor, drawing an image out of a rock, letting the details and patterns in the stone reveal the sculpture hiding within its structure. Everything we build and create is an uncovering. Like a sculptor, we unveil the possibilities in front of us, around us, and within us. All we need to do is discover them. Tune in. Explore. Recognise. Trust. This reminds me of a quote I saw in a social media post: "Your soul knows the answer. You just have to be quiet enough to hear it and brave enough to listen." (Author unknown.)

Quiet. Brave. Listen.

The quote intrigued me. I stopped. I replaced my urge to act, think, and *do,* and listened to my soul. I discovered I can trust my soul. There's nothing to fear. It was as if my soul said, "I got this. You just sit back and relax and let me call the shots." I could feel my soul inside me and around me and leaned into it. It was a physical sensation.

The same applies for whatever you desire to create or build, as well.

Exercise – Lean into Your Creation

Imagine you can lean into the awareness of your completed creation—anything you imagine yourself creating—as if it's already there. Try sensing the energy. It resembles the "being there" people talk about when teaching you to manifest. In addition, there's an element of exploring. Physically (if you can imagine that). I know, it's a bit of a tricky one. Try it. See what you get.

Was it hard? You might have to pretend you understand everything is energy. Consider this: Energy is physicality also in its most subtle form. Your soul is energy. Your soul holds the knowledge of all, including the results of your creation—past and future. Your soul can connect to the energy of your completed creation. When you tap into your soul's wisdom, you can feel that energy. You can recognise the creation as if it's already part of your life.

Too much? Don't worry. Again—you don't have to accept what I say. Investigate. Be curious. Here's a meditation that might help you:

Meditation – Lean into Your Creation

Think about something you want to create. Move your body a little. Lean back. Ask yourself, "Can I sense something? Anything?" Tune in with your finest inner ear (or whichever sensory instrument works for you). Listen. Sense. Discover. Amuse yourself. Play! (Our souls love to play.) Let whatever it is you wish to create guide you. In your imagination, create a picture of what you want and then explore its energy, its vibration. Wonder at the structure, colour, sound. Give it your full attention. Then let the image guide you to your first steps towards creating it. Start with a tone, a word, or a line. See where it takes you. Your soul knows.

That last paragraph reminded me of two things. First, I remembered a phrase one of my spiritual teachers shared in her online course: "You are an infinite, creative being in a body."[2]

Infinite.

Creative.

------

2 Christie Marie Sheldon, Unlimited Abundance, https://www.mindvalley.com/abundance.

What do these words mean? They mean, of course, that you're more than you think you are, and your physical body is only an aspect of you. They also mean you can create anything you want in your life. You can create your life in any way you choose. There's no limit to the possibilities.

Why don't we get on with it, then? Why do we limit ourselves? The teacher also reminded the course participants how we have learnt limitation and restriction from the day we were born. (Probably as early as in our mothers' wombs.) We not only inherit physical traits from our ancestors—we pick up belief systems, emotional patterns, and energies, too. From society we learn what acceptable behaviour is and how a person can and should develop. We even learn how to age. Let me explain:

As I opened to my intuitive and healing abilities, I focused my intention on helping other people release old patterns and trauma so they could heal and come closer to their nature and truth. It led me to starting a practice where I work with clients, individually or as couples. With the same focus as when I listen for the tones, sense my energy, and "lean into" my dreams, I tune in to their souls' images and energies and invite them at a deep (or high, as it were) level—from their heart and soul—to start or continue their healing journeys. The images appear to my inner vision as if in a dream, bringing forward important messages and information. It's satisfying and healing work both for my clients and myself. Every time I work with a client, I experience revelations that help me see more of the magic and wisdom that lies "out there" and in our souls, waiting for us to find them.

The other day, one of these clients asked me to look at her beliefs around her age and the possibility of her becoming a mother. As I tuned in to her soul and vibration, I discovered that beyond the convictions her society had instilled in her, her timeline was uniquely hers. "Isn't everyone's timeline 'uniquely theirs'?" you might ask. Yes. And no. In our world we put certain frames on our life span and its phases that affect the way we think about ourselves and our possibilities—at any stage in our life. We learn that our physical and mental rhythms follow a certain pattern according to the number of years we've walked the earth. Our belief systems teach us we crawl, reach puberty, lose fertility, age, and die at certain ages. These are indisputable facts, it seems, as statistics confirm these convictions. However, this is an illusion. It's a belief we've taken on from society rather than from our true selves.

The image I saw as I tuned in to my client showed a timeline that stretched out in a unique tempo. It revealed how she could allow herself to live in alignment with her nature and follow her natural pulse. With Love. Not because she was different but because she was *she*. She'd adopted, in mind *and* body, society's ideas on aging and bodily changes and thus neglected her own personal rhythm. She'd lost sight of who she was and how she could choose to grow, develop, and even conceive. It was a powerful message that reminded me of how we lock onto "constructed" belief systems created by someone other than ourselves, especially when most of humanity absorbs them as well. I say "most" because there are always a few exceptions. The common feature for those who do things differently is that they refuse to accept the spoken truth. Good for them. Good for us, too. We can follow their example. If we dare to.

Accepting established beliefs about who and what we are without question might cause us to miss our truth—who we are in essence—and forget that we are free to create our lives in our own way. (If we hold on to the love in our hearts and trust our souls.)

My second reflection was new: I wondered how it is we humans have created so many amazing (and destructive) things, all the while rejecting our infiniteness. Those of us who accept our infiniteness appreciate that the power and wisdom of our eternal souls ignite our creations. Yet, in modern times, our creativity has come into play whether or not we embrace the idea that we have a soul. So, you see, our soul is also present during our denial. Everything we create is proof of this.

It touches the realm of magic, doesn't it? We have the art of da Vinci and Michelangelo, the music of Bach and Beethoven, and the pyramids and other wonders. But there's also the computer and the internet, and both enable us to organise our lives in amazing ways and communicate across the globe.

(I remember laughing at this as a young girl, when someone fantasised about the possibility—"in ancient times," as a young person today would say.) This creativity has provided us with the wheel, the sailboat, the aeroplane, and all the machines we use to make our lives easier in the household and on the farm. And we continue to create because as we realise how our old inventions destroy our planet and our lives, people seek ways to ease and mend the destruction—from ways to devour plastic and clean the oceans, to ways of growing sustainable, healthy food without poisonous pesticides. We never stop. We can't. It's part of who we are: infinite, magical, creative beings in a body.

The ferry will soon arrive at the port in Oslo, so I will continue later. First, let me leave you with a small exercise. It won't take long….

Meditation – Listen to Your Soul – I

Soften your eyes. Bring your awareness to the centre of your chest—your heart centre. Imagine all your energy stems from this centre. Let the energy radiate like a big, warm sun through your body and beyond, as far as you can imagine. Can you feel it? If not, pretend you can. Bring out the playful child in you. Can you see it in your mind's eye? This is your soul. Now, imagine sensing your soul as your guide, your greatest mentor. Ask it a question—big or small. Listen. Can you hear anything? Perceive anything? The answer might come as an idea, a thought that rings true, or a sign. Look up. What's the first thing you notice? Is it a sign? Play with it. Be amused. Your observation might amaze you…

The topic of energy has been prominent in my world, returning again and again—different every time—and I would like to explore it with you. First, let me reveal one more thing: I'm a healer. Yes. You can't get more "New Age" than that, I suppose. You can't get more ancient, either. Or unlimited, come to think of it. You can't get more "natural," in fact, as healing with energies is our nature. Because energy is what we're made of, right?

In my healing work, I've become attuned to sensing energy: the dense energy in an elevator filled with a couple who have just quarrelled, for instance, or the light and uplifting energy in a room filled with happy, laughing friends. I've also become attuned to the energies in my body, emotions, and mind.

For instance, when I'm disappointed or angry, I'm tense. My body feels a heavy, dense energy. When my heart overflows with love for someone, or when I'm optimistic and happy, my heart lifts and my body tingles with the incredible, light energy of joy. It can make me run faster than normal—much faster than when I cram my body with self-judgement, guilt, or fear… (Anger is interesting, though. An amazing side effect of anger is that it can also give you speed.)

And the heavy energy? The heavy energies might not be as helpful or fun, but make no mistake, they are just as impactful….

My beloved Fredrik,

I'm not sure I've told you, but when you come home feeling "low," maybe from an upset at school, I pick up on your heavy energy. I become irritable and tired. My mind gets clogged up and foggy. I have to take a breath and, with enhanced awareness, shift my focus, and release the heaviness. Ah, the magic that happens when I remember to do this! I feel lighter, the fog lifts, and I can hug you and give you the love you need. The best part is that when I change my energy, your energy changes, too. You might put it down to a more rational explanation of having been hungry or tired, but I've seen it happen often enough to recognise it as true magic. You know what I'm talking about, don't you? I think you do. It goes both ways, by the way: you pick up on my energies too, although you might not be aware of it. Yet.

I've said it before: We. Are. Connected. We are powerful. It's exciting because when we realise how our energies move, shift, and influence our surroundings, we can help not only ourselves but also other people and our relationship with them.

"How do you shift your energy?" you ask. Well, that's one thing I've learnt. (Or remembered. It's our nature, after all.) Then I practised for a few years, both within myself, and in my work with other people. At first, healing other people was easier than sensing my own energies. I resisted tuning in to myself, still frightened of discovering I was a fraud—ugly, within and without, and filled with patterns (that were impossible to do anything about) and trauma. Traumas that would take me to an awful place if I looked at them.

Today we know our brains cannot distinguish between imagined or remembered experiences and the actual experiences. We understand how repeating a trauma can enhance and solidify the trauma in our systems, body, mind, and soul. The teacher who taught me about my infinite creativity also reminded her students that, "What you give energy to, you re-energise."

Can you guess where I'm going with this? Exactly. It might be helpful and an important part of your healing to look at the trauma from your past. To understand. To discover how the trauma affected your emotions, choices, and sense of worth—and still does. To learn that your trauma is not the essential you. To uncover how you can release it and rise from it. But… Yes, there's a "but." If you keep giving focus, energy, and attention to those traumatic experiences and stories, you re-energise them. You give them power, solidify them, re-enforce them, and tell your mind, body, and entire system you're still in danger, that it's still happening to you. Once you've recognised and acknowledged the hidden trauma in your system, you must shift your focus. "How easy is that?" you might ask. Not easy at all. Yet, it's simple. Let me show you:

Exercise – Shift Your Focus

Find something in your surroundings on which to fix your gaze. Focus on it. Give it all your attention. Notice its colours, shape, size, texture, sound (if any), its placement in the room, anything you can perceive. Then move your eyes to another object. Now give this your full attention and notice its colours, shape, size, texture, sound (if any), its placement in the room, and its relationship to the previous object. Shift your focus between these two objects, giving them your full attention, one at a time. Do this repeatedly—on your own impulse and in your own time. You choose when you want to focus on which object, and how much time you want to give each one. It's an act of your will. It's a choice.

Your choice.

Then bring a touch of magic into the practice, some Tender, Loving Care (TLC). Focus on the first object with curiosity and love. Pretend it's your favourite thing in the world. You love this thing. (It doesn't matter if you do. This is just for fun.) Do the same with the second object until you feel the love as strongly as you did for the first object (or stronger). Little by little, or in one big go, let go of the first object and bring all your TLC to the second object. That's the object of your attention for the rest of this exercise. You've made your choice. Thank yourself, and smile.

Do you get it? Was it easy? Maybe it was. Maybe it wasn't. Was it simple? Of course it was. You know how to shift your gaze and bring your full attention to something when you choose to do so. (If you're not a visual person, you can listen instead. Or feel. Any way you choose. It's all up to you.) Let's try one last thing....

Meditation – Shift Your Focus

Bring your full attention to an object, event, or thought pattern that has caused you frustration. This could be anything. Only you are aware of what's going on in your life. Focus on this one thing. Investigate the sensation, images, or words. Explore the total experience and how it affects your mind, body, and emotions. Try to discover as many sensations as you can, or concentrate on one. How does it affect your body, your heart, your mind?

Then, at a moment you choose, snap your fingers. Search for something in your life, memory, or surroundings that gives you joy—something you truly appreciate. Pick the first thing that comes to mind. Focus. Examine: What is it? Where is it? How does it play out? How does it feel? What can you do with it? Investigate. Notice the emotions, sensations, and experiences, mind, body, and soul.

If you can't identify anything that brings you joy, make something up. Have you ever daydreamed? Now would be a good time to pick up that habit. If a heavy sensation creeps in on you and distracts you (or hijacks you), notice and bring your focus back to the good sensations. Be kind. Don't force it. Don't "try" to be joyful. Allow the joy to fill you. Allowing is light. Playful. Open. Like your soul. Observe the object of your investigation. You chose it because you like it. That's all.

When you're finished, take a moment to reflect on the difference between the two experiences. Can you acknowledge how much lighter the things you appreciate feel in your system than the ones that frustrate you do?

You might stumble upon an obstacle here. Your mind wants to remind you that life can't be all good and lovely. You must remember all those difficult and uncomfortable things so you can prepare yourself for future challenges.

Don't worry. Your mind is trying to keep you safe. You gave it power to do so the moment you forgot the power of your soul. Thank your mind for caring. Remember, your mind is your tool. It doesn't have to be your master. Repeat the statements below. This is important. Don't skip it. Spend time on the statements until you fathom the power of these messages:

"I'm allowed to experience joy."
"I can spend time on what I like."
"I can explore and indulge in the delicious sensations that come with the joy."

We've been living in self-punishment too long. It doesn't get us to a good place. How can it? It's time we practise joy instead. It's time we replace fear and pain with the love and excitement of being alive. Of being us.

I discovered one more thing in relation to this "healing-the-trauma" business. Emotions are energies of different densities, like the intensity of the heat from a fire or the gentle sensation of a warm breeze against your skin. I realised that looking closer at my old experiences wasn't dangerous. For various reasons and in varying ways, the experiences caused tension and pain, but now I recognised them as only that: experiences. Some install better (lighter) energies, and some poorer (denser) energies. Some evoke more fear than others. These experience-installed emotions can shift. You can release them. The old traumas can become less frightening.

With these new realisations, the traumas shifted by themselves. I noticed, acknowledged, and accepted them, then let them go. (To a certain extent.) The last revelation came when I understood, deep within, that these old experiences were *in the past*. I'm not in the past. I'm here, now. The past is gone. Only when I re-energise an experience with my thoughts will it continue to exist in my inner world. I can choose differently. I can choose to let go and be here, now. It's quite simple.

Do my words encourage you, or do they provoke you? Either way, it's okay. You choose what to make of it all. However, before you discard the ideas I just laid before you, I invite you to investigate further. Here's an exercise for you:

Meditation – Listen to Your Soul - II

Contemplate:
Everything is energy. Emotions are energy. Energy moves.

My experiences and traumas have instilled emotions in me.

I can move them. They are in the past.

The past is gone. I can release it.

Now explore:
What emotions do these statements evoke in you? Anger? Resentment? Fear?

Do you blame yourself for not "getting it"? Do you agree? Disagree? Do the phrases confuse you? Disturb you? Or do you feel a sense of relief—excitement, even?

Listen to yourself, not to other people (including me). Lean into your soul. Let it guide you. Focus on your heart. Tune in. Listen. Ask yourself, "Is this true? Or is it a lie?" Remember the difference between the light energies (truth) and the heavy ones (lies). How do the words above affect your body? That's your clue.

If you still disagree with the statements you explored in this exercise, discard them. If you feel confused, don't worry. Leave the contemplations for now. Your soul will let you sense what your truth is. If the statements ring a bell for you, study them further. Inside you. Whatever your case, give yourself a hug. Acknowledging a truth doesn't mean you've solved the mystery. Not necessarily. We're human, after all. We're here to explore this world and navigate in this physical reality. Why? Good question. When I have the answer—the one and only truth—I'll let you in on it. I don't believe it has anything to do with punishment, though. I don't think we're meant to punish ourselves (for whatever reason) and linger in our pain. Nor do I believe there's a higher entity that will punish us if we don't live "the right way." My belief is that we're meant to live from joy and excitement. Expansion and freedom. Love.

I'm inviting you to bring your soul, your essence and light, into your life, and to rediscover who you are. Be patient. Be kind to yourself—and to others. If the revelations I share are unfamiliar, it might take time to absorb them (the ones you choose to absorb, of course). You're still human. You still have to navigate this strange reality. You still need practical human skills, even as you open to a greater awareness. It takes time to shift your reality, but don't worry. What you search for you will find. When you listen, you will hear. When you don't do either, your soul will work with dedication and love to bring your truth to you, anyway. It might take days, weeks, months, years—lifetimes, even (if you don't listen). But you will get to the heart of your being. I said it before: your soul will not fail you. All you need is your intention. Your soul will take care of the rest. Choosing to search and listen will let you in on the secrets faster, though. Just a tip....

I went through training to discover these things. I signed up for various courses dedicated to help people rediscover their natural healing and intuitive powers, and I increased my skills by opening to clients. I practised. I explored. It took time to grasp it, to live it, to understand how energy moves. Discovering how to shift energies (not to mention your perception of reality) takes investigating. And faith. Heavy, dense energy moves slowly. It can keep you in the dark until you can't take it anymore and do something different. In that instant, you shift.

But what if you get stuck? What if you can't get yourself to do something new? Ask for help—from another person, or from yourself. Ask, "What will it take for this to shift? What will it take to replace these heavy energies with lighter, more joyful ones?" Remember, emotion—energy—moves. No matter how dense or how restricted it is, it moves. It's a law of physics. Allow energies to move through your body. Don't stuff them in there. You don't need to. You can let the heaviness go.

In these past few days, I've studied the effect my thoughts have on my energies' density. I've observed how other people's emotions (energies) affect mine. This is all we need to discern to shift our realities. What a delightful realisation!

Now, our life stories have taught us how to live as human beings, and we've all learnt different things. Your caretakers' and society's ways of dealing with practical, social, emotional (and so on) realities taught you how to deal with life—practically, socially, and emotionally—whether you copied them or opposed them. This is a fine thing to discover, though it can be daunting. Through the years, you've learnt from numerous teachings, and a multitude of people have affected your journey. Do you have to look at all these lessons and experiences to decipher what rings true and what you should let go of? Do you need to know every little detail and understand them all? I'm not so sure anymore.

When I heal other people, I tap into the stories of the soul in front of me at a higher level. ("Higher than what?" you might ask. Higher than our everyday human level. A higher vibration. I'll get back to this.) I discovered what aspects had created the patterns, emotions, and beliefs that were inhibiting or hurting the soul—the person. Then, with a bit of real magic and energy (this is what healing is about), I could help them release these old patterns. This is exciting, interesting, and rewarding work. I love it. But I work for one hour at a time. If you have a soul with a lifetime of tough, traumatic experiences, and then, if you believe (as I do) that several lifetimes of experiences have affected our soul, this work is going to take a long time. We're talking hundreds of years.

However, if you accept that all these experiences have created an energy in your system, your physical, emotional, intellectual, and energetic system (Yup, New Age…), then all you must do is tune in, discover the energy, feel the density, notice what part of your system it's attached to (body, mind, heart, or energy field), and release it. Try it for yourself:

Exercise – Release Tension

Notice any tension or density in your body, or any repeating thoughts that disturb your peace of mind. Then choose one of the following exercises—or do all of them.

- Shake it off. Literally. Shake your body. Then take a step to the side, as if you're stepping out of your present state.

- Wave it off. Use your hands and wave it away. Then bring your awareness to your heart and imagine a sun radiating from your heart centre out through your body.

- Imagine the energy's colour. Use your imagination and let the energy's colour flow out like a breeze or a stream until a new colour replaces it.

- Shower it off. Pretend that an energy shower—a shower of liquid light—washes it off, like when you take a shower after a day working in the garden and the dirt runs off your body. (You can do this while you're in the actual shower. Use the sensation of the cleansing water to support the energetic rinse.)

- Shift your focus. Snap your fingers and think about something you like (remember the "Shift Your Focus" exercises?)

In other words: release and replace. Cleanse your system and allow your natural vibration to fill you up. Then give that energy your full attention. Nourish and re-energise your essence instead of those stories that hold you down.

A friend of mine laughed the first time he saw me wave my hands to shake off some dense energy I didn't want anymore. It worked, though. His smirk couldn't change that. With practice, I've become attuned to energy nuances, and I can feel energies move when I ask them to (often like a shiver through my body). Sometimes I do the internal work (the way I'm showing you through this book) and sometimes I look for help beyond myself, whether with the help of other people or something else. Vacuuming, for instance, makes me furious—unless I get ahead of myself, *shake off* the energy, put on some dance music, and have fun instead. Music is a great "external" energy shifter, as are nature, animals, the loving support of a friend, a good film, or anything else you enjoy.

Let's try another exercise:

Meditation – Shake off Disturbances

Bring your attention to something that makes you uncomfortable—a person, an experience, something you must do. Notice the heavy feeling or disturbing emotion the thought of it gives you. Now, instead of blaming yourself—or another person—for making you feel this way, and instead of spending all your energy trying to figure out why you're reacting this way, and what in heaven's name you're repeating those patterns for, just notice. Observe.

Imagine your body surrounded by a bubble of light. Imagine you can see the colour or colours of this light. This is your energy field. (It's common knowledge that we radiate warmth—hence, energy. It's often referred to as your aura). This field is an extension of you. It's also you, just as your body is. Use your hands to shake or push the uncomfortable energies out of your system, out of your body and out of your energy field. Straighten your back, lift your head, and imagine looking above the horizon, as if you have the perspective of a bird. (Or an angel, if you wish.)

Play with this. Have fun with it. Don't try to make sense of it. Notice the sensations....

Now, try something else. Something fun:

Exercise – Shift Water

Take a sip of water. Can you feel the energy of the water as it enters your body? Is it light and nourishing, or does it make you feel heavy? Then hold the glass in front of you and repeat with intention: "I love you" three times, as if you're speaking to the water.

Take another sip. Observe. Has anything changed? Is it lighter? Softer? Or not?

Be curious—this is interesting information. Don't you agree?

Beloved,

Remember the other day when we were sitting at the table talking about intuition? About making choices? How we know which choice is best for us, and why we make a choice we know is not the best one? We were talking about that friend of yours. The one who left the country. I asked you to observe whether there was a distinct sensation to the phrases, "I will meet her again" and "I will not meet her again." You said you felt a "downward" sensation; a denser energy to one phrase, and an upward sensation to the other. You said the downward sensation was a "No," and the upward one was a "Yes." You even put a colour to the different "answers." You were listening to your intuition—your clairvoyance, the part of your reality that takes place in what we, in our linear disposition, call a "future."

You're so wise, Fredrik. You're an inspiration to me, with your curiosity and profound reflections.

This morning, whilst getting ready to go into town for a meeting, I was inspired to share a short, profound message for you to absorb as you move through your day:

Body and Soul – A Reflection

Consider this. You're a high-vibrational soul who has manifested in a physical reality as your body. Your body is the densified aspect of you. It is you. You are your body and everything else. A soul. Your body speaks to your soul, and your soul speaks to your body.

Consider that.

Got to dash!

ll my life I've let my mind roam. It used to disturb me big time. I couldn't focus or concentrate, and all the speculations and worries that came up would overwhelm and confuse me. I'd be churning about an issue with another person, an issue with myself (which, as you understand from my story, was not very uplifting), an issue with life (mostly my life), and so on. My mind was my biggest enemy—a destructive tool. Yet it functioned as fast as could be. Sometimes, other people, threatened or intimidated by the intensity and speed of my thoughts, would ask me to relax and chill. I couldn't. I was a slave to my over-active mind.

My mind continues to work in high gear, but now I enjoy it. (Most of the time.) How? The answer is simple, almost cliché: I meditate. Daily. It's not a new concept. Time and again we hear researchers and gurus reminding us of the benefits of meditation to our minds and our general well-being.

I meditate once a day, often more. Every morning, I set off twenty minutes for meditation, sometimes longer. I meditate whilst sitting on the ferry or in a train, and whilst walking the dog. Sometimes I meditate before I sit down and write, and sometimes when I play the piano—listening to the tones as they flow, one after the other. I meditate when I'm in or near water: the lush sensation of water flowing around my body and the sound of the water flowing in a stream calms me every time. I meditate when I experience tension or overwhelm, when I'm stressed or irritable, or when I long to tap into myself, regain my balance, and enjoy those good vibes.

Meditation has become second nature to me, like breathing. It hasn't always been this way. In the beginning, when I started my healing training—my "reawakening"—I only meditated twice a week, in a group. I found it hard. Because guess what? My mind kept disturbing me. Churning in that old familiar way. It took time before I could enjoy and indulge in the need and desire to meditate. It was only when I shifted my focus, through my process of opening to my soul and learning to sense energies, that my mind could become an amazing tool for discerning and understanding my life and who I am, who we are, and how and why we function the way we do. Now I can glimpse my greater truth. I don't need to stay with the convictions that don't serve me. I can recognise when I need to reconnect, and act upon it.

My mind still runs away with me from time to time, strengthening some old, limiting belief system. But often, as I let my mind be the tool that can help me convey my intuitive insights—through words, colour, and sounds—I find it adds a deeper quality to my intuitive experiences. Spurred on by the images my soul brings forward as it guides me through life, my mind ignites new ideas that lead to new intuitive insights (or reminders, as nothing is new to the soul), and a beautiful soul-mind-dance emerges. When I let it. When I listen.

When I'm not writing this manuscript, for instance, my mind keeps roaming, sometimes covering so much ground I'm afraid I'll lose my way and forget important messages. But then, because I'm getting to be a wise woman, I tell myself, "Hey, don't worry. Just write. The words will come, and whatever comes in the moment is perfect for that moment. What is important will come up again."

The ferry has arrived, and my time with you must end for today. Let me leave you with a simple meditation. You can do this anywhere, anytime. It only takes a moment:

Meditation – Take Three Breaths

Take a deep breath. Let the air drop all the way down into your tummy. Let it flow in without trying too hard. Allow. Allow the air to leave your body on your exhale. Relax.

Take another deep breath. Imagine you're gathering your entire self into the centre of your being, into your body. Breathe in your energy, your soul, your essence. Don't try to understand. Just imagine.

Breathing out again, imagine anchoring all the aspects of you into your hips. Let them "sink" into your hips and relax. Notice how supported you are.

In one final breath, imagine you can bring the wisdom of your soul into your body with your inhale. Drink it in. Allow your essence to permeate your physical being.

With your exhale, explore what it feels like to lean into that wisdom, into your soul. It's almost a physical sensation. It's subtle, but it's there. Can you feel it?

Welcome the comfort of being close to yourself. Acknowledge how safe you are. Your soul has your back.

One more thing before I leave:

Acceptance...
Accept who you are.
Accept where you are, now, in this very moment.
Try it. It's delightful.

Yes, acceptance. A tricky concept, yet easy when you get it—and rewarding. It's a special sensation. Once you've recognised it, you can utilise it at will. The trick is remembering to return to it.

Many people have had the experience of getting something "right" the first time (we don't call it "beginner's luck" for nothing), and then struggling to do it—whatever it is—the second time. (Often without success, I might add.) The first time I went bowling, for instance, I got one strike after another and won the game. (I was the only rookie.) The second time, I couldn't get one hit! Why? You probably know the answer: I was trying to succeed, so I failed. My "humanness" impeded nature. The flow escaped me.

At first, when I started writing this book, the words flowed. The first day, and the next. Because I let them. Then I struggled, trying to control the flow. I worried about missing something, and tried to remember and hold on to the thoughts that came to me when I was out walking, or meditating, or when I was cleaning the house. I recorded ideas on my phone or jotted them down on a piece of paper, only to forget I'd done it. I felt stressed and tense about the book. *Was it all a mistake?* Remember how I tried to have fun playing the piano but got tired instead? It was much the same experience. However, the moment I let go of the worry and sat down at my computer with curiosity and an open mind, the words flowed again. My energy increased. I had fun.

All I had to do was allow—accept and trust the process, and let the words find their way into the book. My intuition—my soul—knows what to say.

Acceptance. Presence. Flow.

My dearest Fredrik,

Do you remember that not long ago someone asked me to play a piece at the 100th anniversary at your school? I was thrilled! It was my first opportunity to do something new, something different from what everyone expected. I wanted to play my music, to play the tones that came to me intuitively in the moment. To allow the flow. My flow. I'd be honouring the traditions of the school by bringing a tune they would recognise into the improvisation, maybe, but in my way. All on my own. I'd never done it before, but I knew I could do it. I trusted it. Do you recall what happened? I tuned in to the atmosphere, listened to my inner guidance, and played. It was perfect. It was different from when I had tried it by myself in my studio, yet it was perfect because I created it there and then—in the moment. I tuned in and allowed the flow—accepting what came— because I'd chosen to do so.

Yes. We can choose. We are that powerful.

I'll get back to this—there's more to say about this topic.

PART II
MASTER YOUR LIFE

When your path takes a turn
you had not expected,
what can you do?
You can accept.
If it takes you back to a moment in the past,
you can revisit it
and learn from it.
You can rejoice at the opportunity
to deepen your wisdom of that which was.
If you wish.
It's all up to you.

May 24 – Three Years Later, at the
kitchen table in our little home once more

Dearest Fredrik,

I confess: I've neglected you. More accurately: I've neglected sharing my story with you. For three years, I've been absent from this manuscript. You might notice this as you read on; you might not. My tone might be different now, after two years of the pandemic and a global shutdown, and then a year of trauma and life-changing illness in our family after your father suffered his stroke. You witnessed the incident, and though he survived, he still suffers the consequences. It was a severe stroke. I know it frightened you. In the two years that followed, you and I had to find our way together through fear and grief. You had to be more courageous than ever before in your young life, and I had to be as strong as I could be both for you and your father. It wasn't easy. You had to release the shock from your system, and I had to do my best to keep you as safe—and myself as nourished—as I could whilst searching to become a freer, more authentic, happier human being. And a better mother to you.

Time alters things. I'm not the same person I was three years ago. Neither are you. Last year's events shook our reality to the core. The past few years have shaken the world, too. Many things have changed. Or have they?

Here I am, eager to continue sharing my experiences and exploring the wisdom that comes to me as I keep searching and growing. I'm sitting at the same kitchen table in the same little house, with the same oak tree outside our window.

Sometimes, it's as if the pandemic never happened—that when it comes down to it, nothing has changed, in us or in the world, and that everything remains the same. The events of these years might have scratched the surface and taught us a lesson. Perhaps we grew and developed somewhat, but at the core, we continue to be ourselves, right? Our soul still carries the essence of our being. Yet, when I look back, I feel different from only a few years ago. It's as if I've shed an old coat. I feel stronger, freer, warmer, and wiser. Not because of the pandemic or the family trauma, but because of my never-ending search for the truth and my essence. I'm inclined to believe I've found the fountain of youth(fulness).

I can't remember why I left my words hanging those three years ago—there might be plenty of reasons. I might have fallen into the trap of trying: trying to be creative and clever, trying to share something of importance. (Yay! We're back on the topic!) Why is "trying" disturbing to our flow? Where does it come from? From fear, of course. Fear of not being good enough or valuable enough in and of ourselves. Fear that the flow is not enough, and that we have to prove to the world we are worthy of love.

Beloved Fredrik,

A memory comes to me as I write these words. It might clarify how powerful fear can be: I was in the hospital after having given birth to you. It was the most intense, magical, and exhilarating event in my life, but I was struggling. There was no milk. No matter how much I wanted to and how hard I tried, I could not nurse you. I called the nurse. She was Swedish, I remember, with that certain energy only Swedish women can muster. I can't explain it; you must experience it. I shared my concern with her, and she said (in her very Swedish way, drawing out the "aaaah" in the Swedish sing-song-version of the Scandinavian word for "Yes"): "Jaaaaaa. You see," she said (all in a very Swedish way), "when you're afraid there will be no milk, the flow will stop. Like this." She showed me what she meant. She walked to the sink in the corner, turned on the tap forcefully, then shut it down again, stopping the flow of water in much the same way I was doing with my milk, apparently, because I was worrying (a sneaky cousin to fear) about being the one woman in the world who could not feed my son. (For the record: once I got it, the milk wouldn't stop. And then you drank as if your life depended on it—which it did).

This is how inhibiting our fear is. It can stop the flow of nature itself. Which applies to our creative flow as well, of course: it too is nature. When we allow it to flow. When we don't try to prove we are good enough. Creative. Powerful.

Indeed, fear might be the reason I stopped writing this book three years ago. It might also be this: One day, as I sat at my computer, I received a message from my mother about a beautiful chateau in France we had visited once. It was for sale. My response? "All we have to do is win the lottery." It was a joke, but at the same moment an ad popped up on my computer: an ad for the lottery. It was too funny. I bought a lottery ticket. I didn't win, but it was a point of no return. These ads come into my mailbox every once in a while, but this time it woke me up to something that was already brewing in me—something new, fresh, and enticing: my Big Vision.

Was it a sign? Maybe not, but my choice to see it as one was a sign in itself. A sign from my higher or inner self. I was responding to the coincidence because I wanted to, and that's all that matters. We're all the orchestrators of our own lives.

From that point on, my vision developed and took form, until one day I called a friend who knew more about building a business and dealing in property and finance than I did. I wanted to show him my idea. We met. I presented my idea. "Is it workable?" I gave him a rough estimate of the money I would need to raise. "That's not a lot of money," he said. "I'll talk to a business friend." A hug, a big smile on my face, a spring in my step: this was exciting. I knew I had started something important and was certain my Big Shift was just around the corner. I had practised asking the Universe to bring me all kinds of things—small things—and the result was convincing. I was confident the Universe (or whatever it is) listens and responds. Why not for my Big Vision, too? It was a grand vision—for children, humanity, peace, and the world. Why wouldn't the Universe bring it to me? I walked to the cinema where I was meeting a friend to see a film I'd been part of. On the way there, I received a text from the film producer. The cinema had to shut down. It was Friday, March 13, 2020, the day the pandemic shut-down started in my country.

Little did we know then that for two years we would all be sitting still, or raging, or worrying, or crying out in grief (or all the above) while we waited to see what this COVID-19 was going to do to us. Would it kill us? Was it a message from higher forces? Was it planted? Was it our fault? Was this our opportunity to change the world? Should we despair? Relax? Spend time with our loved ones? Tear out our hair at having to be with our loved ones all the time? Fight? Pray? Heal? Look for peace? Love? Get a pet? Create?

There were so many questions, opinions, and convictions, and a lot of anger and fear. And for me? I found I had to sit down and try to be present. To find my own convictions. I tried to keep the confusion and fear that gushed out through the media at a distance. It was intense, I remember. I had to work hard to find my voice amidst the noise and recover a place of stillness within. A place of trust. Being.

Many people suffered in the shut-down. In Norway, we were fortunate to live in a society that could care for us—financially—and most of us could move around in our natural environment: the forest, the sea, our garden. It gave me the opportunity to practise the art of Being—an unfamiliar skill for me, as I've spent the greater part of my life *doing* (like most of us).

I must admit—I didn't sit still for very long. I started "doing" once more. Certain things never change. My desire to create, along with my urge to grow and learn, kept me going during the time of confinement. Or because of it. As I mentioned, three years ago, I had started creating music and writing my story of how my perspective—on myself, on my life, and on life per se—had shifted. In addition, there was My Big Vision—the vision that had come to me just before the shut-down. It was a magnificent dream—a dream of creating empowering peace centres all over the world for the young generation and their parents to come and heal, tap into their worth and strength, and express their passion and wisdom through the arts. I couldn't ignore that idea.

To summarise: Though I neglected finishing this book, I spent the shut-down creating and developing a great idea. I also released an album with my music (yay!), and I shared my insights and experiences on (the crazy, sometimes magnificent, sometimes disturbing) social media. All the while, I was exploring and coming closer to my truth, my essence. Home.

The shut-down lasted two years. Two years. It's hard to fathom today, when the world has picked up its maddening pace again. Don't you agree? You might ask, "Where will our world end?" Time will tell, I suppose, though I believe the world will change. I believe the souls who are being born now will see to it. That's why I'm determined to fulfil my vision. I want to be part of the shift.

There you have it. Three years without writing. Then, out of the blue, a friend and mentor advised me to write a book.[3]

---

[3] Patrick Chassagne of Melcion, Chassagne & Cie, https://melcion.com.

(You never know where the next brilliant idea will come from, so keep your eyes and ears open, and listen.) We were in a coaching session when he surprised me with the idea. It reminded me of the voice that whispered in my ear years ago. Later, I opened a blank document and started from the beginning. I knew I'd been contemplating writing a book before, but I'd erased the first manuscript from my mind. As I went to save the first draft of my new document, I found another document with the same name. I opened it to see what notes and comments I might have put in it. It was the book I had started three years ago. The words captured me, and I picked up where I'd left off.

I've taken gigantic steps on my journey since last time I wrote, and my sense of magic, purpose, alignment, and awareness is in a different place today. I'm stronger. I'm more grounded. I know who I am and why I'm here. I'm stubborn in my soul-searching endeavours. I will not rest. (It's a paradox, I realise, as my awareness also shows me it's in the resting—the being—that our essence and Source is available to us. Hmmm. I'm sure I'll "get it" one day.) But I'm still me and I've got things to share—things you might find helpful on your own journey. I hope to find the best possible words, words that will trigger your innate wisdom and curiosity. Follow the flow. That's what I was showing you, wasn't it? I urge you to read the following section with care:

I'm not here to tell you who you are, how to live your life, or what you should believe in. I'm not here to show you what your purpose is or to reveal your truth for you. My greatest wish is that you discover this for yourself. That's where your power lies.

I'm sitting here, by the kitchen table in our little home. It's a cottage, really, with wooden floors, white panelling on the walls, a wood burner, and a large, wonderful, wild garden. The birds love our garden, as do the deer and squirrels. Bella, the puppy we're looking after, loves crawling up into Fredrik's bed in the morning when I bring him a cup of tea. We've been looking after her since we had to part with our big, warm-hearted Lobo—a rescue dog, a husky with one blue and one brown eye. (How I loved that big, clumsy, furry dog. He looked like a wolf—the gentlest wolf you could imagine.) We still live on the beautiful peninsula in the Oslo Fjord, surrounded by the sea, with trees everywhere, and our friends close by. It's been our home for a few years, but our time here will conclude soon. Our home isn't all mine to own and hold on to, and Nicolay, Fredrik's father, needs his share of the money. All things must end.

I want to share some of the experiences, insights, and tools I've gathered on my path. I hope they can be of value to you. Your path is your own. Sometimes it can feel lonely and terrifying. In order to navigate the crossroads, stumbling blocks, or wild shrubbery that blocks our path, sometimes we need a different perspective—a nudge, and some tender, loving care from those who have travelled the road already. Obstacles may seem impossible to overcome, but there's always a way. Once you search, your nature will pull you with unbreakable strength and wisdom towards your release and clarity, your natural state of Love. There's no avoiding it. You just need to search….

Pray, and you shall receive.
Tune in, and you shall hear the answer.
Follow your instinct with curiosity.
Meditate, listen, investigate.
Play, explore, imagine.
Laugh, cry, scream, indulge.
Let it all flow through you. Observe: What is your soul telling you?

I'm getting ahead of myself. There's so much to share and so much to show you….

On my quest to rediscover who I am and open to the magic and the Divine, every effort is worth it tenfold. It's exhilarating to own the experience of who (or what) I am, and to comprehend that I can create the life I choose. This appreciation is more compelling and impactful than fear, frustration, or limiting beliefs can ever be. Those reactive emotions and restraining beliefs were the structures I built around myself, my core, so I could fit in and "be" a human. They're not my only reality.

That about sums it up.

There's more, of course: When I feel into my soul and remember who I am beyond my human structures, I gain access to a limitless Source of wisdom and information. This wisdom is Love. Pure Love. It's all I need to know. It brings me information beyond my human imagination. The source? My true nature. The Divine. Because as a soul I am of the Divine. There's no separation.

When I tune in this way, I'm in alignment. Even my mind collaborates with me, as it recognises the advantage of connecting to that infinite wisdom and information, and it allows me to perceive the wisdom with ease. It's exciting!

With unending possibilities in mind, let me see if I can shed more light on the flow we allow for when we're in alignment. It's a flow free from control and achievement—an almost incomprehensible concept to any human being. Everything our culture has taught us is about achievement. "What do you do? What is your profession? Are you rich or poor? Are you fit? How young can you try to stay? What does your garden look like? What car are you driving? Are you a mother? A father? A husband? A wife?"

These are all cover-ups and distractions from the real accomplishment: how often can you just *be*? My claim is that "being" is the one thing you need to understand if you wish to live a happy, fulfilled life. It doesn't mean discarding your visions, dreams, or goals. It means being present with yourself in every moment as you move through life, whether it be towards a life of vision and purpose or towards the end of a path on your daily morning walk. In other words, it means being present whether you're enjoying the simplest moments in life or seeking happiness in great achievements and sublime wisdom.

I'd like you to sit with the following statements for a while, as they carry a profound message: When you're present with yourself, when you're "being" and you're in alignment, you're connected to your essence. Your essence is of the Divine. It's pure Love. It expands beyond any human concept of control and beyond doing, achieving, or accomplishing. It is—you are—pure energy.

When you're in this energy, when you're connected to it at your core and dare to expand its beautiful light and vibration out and beyond your physical form, you radiate You. You become the fullest expression of yourself. You become the vibration, colour, and timbre that emanate in harmony with the highest, most beautiful vision and purpose your soul can hold. You move with that harmony, and you fill your life with it. Your soul reverberates with all that you are and all you can be and have in your life. With ease and grace. Once you've reached this point of harmony with your entirety, you desire no more. You let go of control and achievement, and experience gifts beyond what you could imagine. Fast. Easy. Naturally. With love.

There are, however, two potential traps we as human beings may fall into when we work to become present—to just "be."

- First, sometimes we look to the rewards that being present in the moment will bring: a better life, abundance, peace, and love. This is a perfect way to miss the point, because when we try to "be" as an accomplishment or a means to an end, we step out of the "being." Remember how I dropped in energy when I was "trying" to play the piano? I wasn't present, and I lost my connection to myself and to the wisdom and music of the moment. I was no longer in alignment. Alignment is "being." No more, no less. It is "being" because that's what we are. We Are. Do you see?

- The second thing we do—once we've moved out of the state of being—is scold and blame ourselves for not being "good enough," "spiritual enough," or "wise enough." Please be kind to yourself. When you lose touch with yourself—with your Home—you need kindness. Love. That's when you're at your most vulnerable, after all. Love this stumbling person more than ever and with all your heart. Do so *because* of the disconnection. Then ask yourself, "What do I want? What's right for *me?*"

It's about what you want, then. Not should want. Not think you want because someone told you so, or because you long for acknowledgement and love. What you want when you're You.

What do you want? Do you know? Can you tell the difference between what you want and what other people think you should want? Can you recognise the tingle inside you—the sense of relief—that comes the moment you find out what you want? There's a specific sensation that will tell you what you want. In the beginning of your search, you might only perceive it faintly, in a flash, but there's no doubt. As long as you're open to discover, it will be available to you.

Meditation – Discover What You Want

Listen. Explore. With curiosity. Investigate as if you're studying an object you don't recognise. As if you're trying to work out what it's for. Ask yourself: "What do I want? How can I recognise it? What does the sensation of my genuine desire feel, sound, smell, and look like? How does it resonate within me when I'm on the track of my soul's vibration and colours? What colours am I comfortable with? What timbre is mine? What is the natural expression of my soul? What aspects of the Universe am I carrying with me on this earth?"

I must dash, but I'll return tomorrow with more on this topic. In the meantime, ponder the questions above. Go deep within. What's calling you from the depth of your heart, asking you to bring it into your life no matter what anyone says? Can you sense it?

My love,

How are you feeling? Do you know what you want—in your heart? For yourself? Body, heart, mind, soul? Can you for one minute forget everything we, your parents, teachers, friends, and society have taught you, and hear the voice of your essence? Do you recognise your own truth—your colours, sounds, vibrations—amidst the noise that surrounds you? Find it, Fredrik. Don't give up. It's there for you, in your heart and soul. Even when you feel confused or fearful. Trust yourself.

I know a wee bit about what not knowing your own mind means. After my initial childhood years of exploration and wonder, I've spent my life trying to figure out what the "correct" thing to want was. What did society—my family and friends included—decide I should want? I had no idea what it felt, smelled, sounded, or tasted like to want something all by myself. I had to investigate.

It goes a little like this: You ask yourself, "What do I want?" Then you walk around trying to "get it." That's all. "Except," you might ask, "what about my mind, which keeps reminding me of the 'right' things I should want? I should want to relax, of course. Or should I? I should want to be healthy. I think. I should want to be kind and generous and rich and successful and spiritual and strong and soft and sexy and fun and loved… Shouldn't I?"

Maybe. Maybe all those things are what you want, but until you know this within yourself, it's something someone has told you that you want. Do you get what I'm talking about? It's tricky, I realise. I'll try to clarify. The moment you recognise feeling at home and safe, when you're content and you catch yourself smiling for no reason, that's when you know.

How do you find that feeling?

You might be brilliant at this already, but please bear with me for a moment. Most of us go through life not knowing what we want in our poor hearts. I'm sure you can find areas in your life where you didn't know if you made a choice from your own truth, or from some belief or pattern someone else installed in you. Let's not allocate blame, though. We all navigate from what we believe. Through our own stories, we try our best to understand the world and to live good lives. But how do we recognise the state of alignment that confirms our choices and actions are in line with our desires, passions, and essence, and not with a misguided belief?

To answer this question, let me share a story. Nay, two stories—one more mundane (and perhaps easier to understand) than the other:

I was sixteen. We—my mother, brother, and I—were living in Santa Barbara, California, USA. My mother was studying at the University of California Santa Barbara (UCSB) for a year. It was Christmas, and we were driving to Los Angeles to visit my dad's cousin Linda, her husband Mike, and their children, Sarah and John. We had spent Christmas with them in my grandparents' home in Norway when I was a child, and they had invited us to celebrate the holidays in their LA home. It was a long drive. There were no iPads, smartphones, or fancy devices to entertain us, only a radio that kept breaking up and shifting channels as we moved along. What could a sixteen-year-old do under those circumstances? Brace yourself. I—of all things—decided I was going to figure out how to move my ears.

Yup.

Move my ears.

That was the thrill of a long drive in those days: the opportunity to practise moving your ears.

Perhaps this says more about me than about those days. (I've never heard of anyone doing this, but I suppose it's not something people talk about.) But there I was, exploring, testing, trying, until… yes! After a couple of hours (I remember the exact moment), I felt my ears moving—I had found the muscle.

Then what? I did it once, and then it was gone. Could I repeat the feat? You got it: I tried again. I kept investigating until… yes! There it was again. After a while, I did it again, and after a shorter while, once more. Finally—in good time before reaching LA—I could move my ears at a whim. My intention was all I needed. My system now knew what "moving my ears" meant and how to accomplish it. Even today, I can muster up that muscle. There's nothing to it. It's become part of my physical nature, you might say. A fun, little trait.

⇛

The next story is not as fun. It's s.e.r.i.o.u.s. It involves the soul, the higher wisdom and… dare I say it? The D.i.v.i.n.e.

Shhhh

I'd reached adulthood, completed my education as a (fearful) pianist, worked as a musician and teacher for a few years, given birth to Fredrik, lived with his dad Nicolay for a number of years, suffered a traumatic break-up, and was on the path to rediscovering my higher self and inner voice. Always on the lookout for greater wisdom, I reached out to a new coach, Ulla Suokko of Wise Woman Energetics,[4] to help me with my career development. Ulla was an "intuitive." One day, her intuition and higher guidance gave her a sentence for me to ponder—a

---

[4]   Ulla Suokko, Wise Woman Energetics, https://wisewomanenergetics.com.

sentence that had a great impact on me: "See yourself with the eye of the Divine." That was it. I repeated it to myself. I wondered at it. But I could not grasp it. I mean, how on earth do you do that? When I got home, I coaxed Lobo into our little car, drove to the forest, and we went for a long walk (as I often do when something boggles my mind). I find walking moves my thoughts, especially the stuck ones. (Have you tried it? You should). This one got stuck.

While walking, I asked myself, *What is the eye of the Divine? Where is it? What does that statement even mean?* I kept walking. Asking. Imagining, searching within, looking at myself from above, from all sides… I tried and tried. I walked and walked.

Until… Yes. There it was—I got it!

It was magnificent.

Pure.

Simple.

Powerful.

Open.

Warm.

Grand.

Clean.

It felt like an instant, all-empowered, pure glance.

It was Love.

With the revelation came this experience (not knowledge or reflection or insight, experience):

I Am.

That's all. There's nothing to forgive or understand. Nothing to try, do, learn, fix, heal. I am. It was the most enlightening experience of coming Home you could imagine. Or not. Because everything simply *is*.

As I drove home, I stopped to buy some groceries. In the store, I asked myself: "What if I look at everyone else in the same way?" Sure enough, the experience was the same: everyone *is*. There's nothing to forgive or understand, nothing to try, do, learn, fix, or heal. *We are.*

That's all.

Wow....

Meditation – See Yourself with the Eye of the Divine

Ponder the statement: "See yourself with the eye of the Divine." Investigate. Look around you. Look within, from above, from below. Practise. Find that muscle. When you do, try again. Find it a second time. A third. A fourth. Until you know it. Until you live it.

I'll leave you with that for now, but I'll be back soon. Because there's more. Much more. After all, we're human beings trying to figure it all out. Until then, remember:

You. Simply. Are.

A new day has dawned....

Is it morning where you are right now? It is where I am: A beautiful, sun-filled spring morning. I woke up in this lush little private suite I rented to indulge in a two-day holiday for myself. A rare treat. Too rare. Please don't follow my example. There's nothing prestigious or "good" about not treating yourself. Neglecting your desire to feel good is a limiting pattern. Break the pattern: start indulging in good things for yourself. Today.

I wanted to continue writing. Notice the keywords: I wanted. I didn't feel I had to, though I admit there was an element of that as well. I feel an obligation and desire to inspire, help, heal if I can. It feels right. That was the clear, simple experience I had this morning. My original plan had been to stay in bed all morning and do nothing (except perhaps drink my tea and read a few pages in the book I grabbed as I left home yesterday). But deciding to write instead was a pure choice from my inner resonance, my essence.

You need to explore, investigate, and search for that resonance to discover it, especially if you're not sure what you want in and of yourself. It's important to remember to be kind and gentle with yourself if you don't "get it" as quickly as you'd like. You're unravelling one of life's biggest and most life-changing mysteries. Once you've dared to open to the magnitude of your wisdom and greatness, you might face a whole new reality. A better one, but most likely an unfamiliar one. You might not be ready. Yet. There might be one or two more steps to take before you can embrace the change. It might not be the right time. Yet. It's natural. Give yourself some slack. Investigate. Be curious. When you're ready, the gates to the experience will open and you'll know what you want. You'll recognise that which resonates with your heart.

The book I'm reading now, for instance, is one of the big successes in the world: Eckhart Tolle's *The Power of Now*. I tried to read it before, but I couldn't get beyond a few pages. It left me feeling a tad slow. It's easy to wonder if there's something wrong with you when your mind gets cluttered and you can't grasp what an author is explaining—especially if their book is deep, influential, and popular. Today I grasped what Mr Tolle is saying. Not because I've become more intelligent since the last time I tried to read it. I was ready. I had already experienced the essence of what he is sharing through his words.

The paradox is that the chapter I'm reading now explains how the mind causes us pain as it works to keep us in a kind of co-dependent relationship with time: with the past and the future (which, as Mr Tolle points out, only exist in the mind). The only way to bypass the mind and live in alignment is to step out and observe the mind's mechanisms, all the while keeping your focus on being in the moment. Which is the only place to be. After all, as we've established, in the eye of the Divine, we simply *are*… Here and now. In and of ourselves.

Then it hit me. How do you bypass your mind? Again, you explore, wonder, look within, and look from above and below, until you get it. Capisci? (Which means "do you understand?" in Italian. It's pronounced "capeeshee." I love that word. It has a delightful sound). I believe Mr Tolle has "got it," and he's trying to show it to us, his readers. We all have access to this wisdom— the sensation, knowing, and experience of the truths of our nature. Still, there are no words, thoughts, or teachings that can install that experience in you. You have to—you can choose to— investigate for yourself. Until you "get it," too.

Why shouldn't you get it if another human being did? You're made of the same stuff as anyone else. Remember, you're an unlimited being in a body. No one is better or wiser than another person in this sense. Some of us have recognised the whisper of our soul and tuned in to hear what it has to say. That's all. You can do this, too. You can allow the pull from within to guide you towards clearer waters so you can float and play and be free. It's a freedom that's available to us all once we've let go of the old, sticky lies that make up our inherited world view.

It's all about coming home, about being you. In essence and life force, in dance and movement, in Love. Being.

It's time for breakfast. Ta-ta for now! Much, much love to you all.

June 2, at home in our little cottage

Hello, my darling, I'm back again.

It's been five breakfasts since I last wrote. It's the first week of June—the first month of summer. My favourite season. This is the time to create, laugh, heal, and play. It's the time to walk barefoot in the grass. It's the time for those quiet mornings by the sea, and to sit outside and enjoy the long, light Nordic evenings. It's also the time when Norwegians step out of their comfortable houses and lift their gazes to meet and greet one another. It's when they strip off those heavy winter clothes to let the sun warm their skin and bring a glow to their cheeks. Summer is the season when Norwegians come alive, spending their time outdoors as often as they can, living life to the fullest before the cold and darkness force them to move back inside.

I hear the birds twittering all around me as I sit on our lovely little terrace. It's been my favourite spot since we had it built two years ago. The garden is gorgeous this time of year—the grass and the trees bright green, the apple tree blossoming, and our lilacs at the height of their colour, their rich fragrance filling the garden. Sadly, we shall have to move soon. We're preparing our home for sale. There was no way around it. All the challenging circumstances of the last few years have led to this. We've had a multitude of beautiful moments here, but it's time to change direction now. Nature is exploding in renewed growth and expansion around us, surrounding the house with magic and beauty. I hope to hand the house off to someone who will love it and treat it well.

I'm a little nervous about this move, as partly, we'll be going different ways: you've decided to live with your dad and attend school in the city, and I'm going back to the territory of my childhood. We're both leaving a community of friends and loved ones and heading for new experiences and opportunities. We'll find our way, and grow from the change, but change is change. It can be daunting. I'll do my best to lean into it and have faith. Your optimism and your confidence that all will be well motivates me, my beloved Fredrik. I hope to be the example that inspires you to thrive.

Life runs away with you sometimes, doesn't it? The next moment we run away with it—carrying it on our backs as we run off to make it in time. In time for what? Exactly. What are we trying to reach? Why these deadlines all the time?

Let me tell you—I've had some mind-blowing experiences of the contrast between having to rush toward something important and realising that none of it matters. The only thing we need to do is explore the moment. We're all in movement—in transition—whether or not we like it, and whether or not we "get it." Every soul on this planet is only here for "a moment." We arrived, and we will leave. Agreed? In the meantime, the earth will continue to circle the sun for billions of years more, and there's nothing we can do about it. But we can explore. We can love. We can uncover the power and bliss that lies within us. We can spend our hours, days, weeks, and months doing whatever it takes to remember who we are and how we can live gloriously in alignment with all that we are. We can search for ways to reconnect to and live from the Love that is our nature. Until we leave this world and reunite with the free and natural flow of our higher being. Then we won't have to search. Then we *know.*

I declare: We're all part of the Divine. We all express the Divine of Creation in our souls. Each soul radiates its unique aspect of Creation. Just as the Divine is the Creator, we too are creators. We are beauty, love, peace, and light. We can ignore this awareness for as long as we wish, but in the end, our souls will always strive to move towards a balanced unity with Creation. With the Divine. It's our nature. Our purpose if you like. Yet we spend our days worrying about little things that, keeping this unity in mind, appear futile. We give power to things that don't matter overall—things that throw us off balance and confuse and disturb us. We continue to do this regardless of whether we recognise how out of kilter we are. We lose sight of our divinity—our nature—precisely because we're confused. Out of balance. We spiral downward and feel the pain of separation from Creation in body, mind, and soul.

There's a remedy: Balance. Yin and Yang. Feminine and masculine. Darkness and light. The dichotomies balance out, and in the end, in beautiful, balanced unity, there is no Yin and Yang, feminine and masculine, darkness and light. The dichotomies become illusions, and our nature restores itself. We *are.*

We're not there yet. Thankfully, because when we've recovered the balance, there will be nothing more to explore, learn, or create. Even as we struggle and strive to regain balance and joy—are we ready to embrace the peace and stillness that follows (I expect) from balance and harmony? I'm not sure, because I, in my humanness, have no way of imagining this balance.

Let's do what we can, then, to create our lives from our hearts. Let's seek peace and balance, while embracing the experience and the journey. Let's unravel our tangled human selves so we can recognise and live from our essence again.

"How?" you ask. Let me share an analogy. I call it The Silk Scarf:

The Silk Scarf – An Analogy

Your dear friend has returned from her travels and brings you a gift from afar: a large, stunning silk scarf. You receive it with gratitude, admiring its softness and beauty. The breeze catches it, nearly pulling it out of your hand. You hold on to it tightly, watching its gentle, wavy movements, its colours radiant in the sun. You wonder at how delicate it feels—almost fragile. A gust of wind tugs at it. The scarf slips through your fingers, floats away, and lands a short distance from you. Its movement mesmerises you. The scarf could fly off into the blue sky, never to be seen again, but you wish to keep it, to feel that lush sensation against your skin. You pick it up and tie a knot in the middle, careful not to tighten it too much. You want it to continue moving in the breeze. You cradle it in your hand.

As your friend leaves, a fear disturbs you. You remember an old threat of having valuable things taken from you, teaching you that you're not worthy of such beauty. You tighten the knot to ensure you won't lose it. The scarf loses its flow. You hold on to it, but its beauty, the wavy movements, the colours, all seem to fade. Soon, your memory of the mesmerizing moment when you first set your eyes on the scarf becomes hazy. Now it's just another scarf. It's lost its magic, and you put it in a drawer with some other clothes.

Time passes, and life goes on. You forget all about the silk scarf. Then, one early summer evening, the friend who gave you the silk scarf comes to see you. You sit together in the garden, relaxing. She asks about the scarf, reminiscing about her encounter with the weaver who sold it to her on her visit to a remote village in a distant country. The woman taught her to value the scarf for its natural radiance and delicate colours. You remember.

You bring out the scarf to show her—a lump of fabric crimped into a tight knot. You barely recognise it.

She looks at it, then at you, and smiles. She takes it from you, unravels it, softens the knot, and flicks the soft fabric outward. The breeze catches it. You watch as it moves, feeling deep respect for the craftswoman who created it. The colours shine, and you recognise the natural flow, the scarf's softness, its beauty. It brings joy to your heart once more.

Do you recognise it? The scarf is you. It's your natural, flowing self: radiant colours, wavy flow, silky feel. When not manifested in your beautiful body, it moved through the air and out into the universe. Then, as you entered this earthly reality, you gathered your flowing self (the scarf) into a denser, though supple and moveable, body. At first, you screamed at the shock of being restricted in your movements. But soon, you were eager to adapt. The larger part of you (your soul) could still dance and flow. The denser part of you (your physical manifestation) could sense, hold, and caress. Until you encountered fear—the fear of not being held, the fear of not being loved. You tightened the knot. You forgot your soul and hindered your flow, creating tension and pain in your body and heart. Then one day, a beautiful soul touched your heart, maybe, and reminded you of who you are, so you could untangle the knot enough to move, shine, and love once more.

This is you. All of you. Body and soul in one transitional Whole.

I'll leave you for now—must get off to the ferry. In the meantime, savour the flavours this image brings to you. Explore them. Feel the truth. Embrace it. Smile. And dance.

t's the middle of the night, and I'm sitting at our kitchen table in my nightgown, a single candle casting a soft light in the room. It's quiet here, in our little corner of the world. No sounds in the night, only the clock ticking away. Even the birds are resting. I'm not sure what woke me up, but soon my mind returned to yesterday's topic, and the voice inside me urged me to sit down and write before I forgot what I wanted to say.

So how do you loosen that knot? How can you allow your energy and colours to flow with ease, revealing all your beauty, and reconnecting you to your unique vibration while expressing yourself through your human "knot" (your body)? It's easy once you "get it." But that's the trick, right? "Getting it." Which is why people are writing and selling books on how to heal and discover your truth. Like this one. Let's try once more. Maybe this time you'll "get it." Maybe this time I'll find the words that will awaken the memory in you. Here's what you can do:

Exercise – Loosen the Knot – I

Stretch. Embrace. Caress.

Your body.

Hold hands with someone. Dip your toes in the water. Walk barefoot in the grass: What are the sensations on your skin?

Reach your arms towards the sun. Smile, laugh, play. What happens to your body, mind, emotions?

Visualise something that brings good vibrations to your body—the taste of a fresh berry, the scents in the forest, a kiss, the soft fur of your pet. Indulge.

Lean back a little. Pay attention to the moment. Where are you? What sounds, smells, colours surround you? Explore.

Go out in the rain and jump in a puddle. Wish upon a star. Climb a tree. Gaze into the fire. Listen to music. Run as fast as you can and notice your muscles as they work to move your body. Put on a gorgeous dress or shirt. Give your child a big, warm, comforting hug. Surprise yourself. Meditate.

Relax.

Do one of these things or all of them. Listen to the pull within, and let your desire guide you. What exercise do you feel like trying in this moment?

Then observe the knot untying, little by little. Perhaps it happens without you noticing at first. Or perhaps it happens in a sudden jolt—if that's your way. If that's your soul's way.

In short, every time you feel joy, contentment, passion, or peace—that's when you soften the knot. It's all you have to do.

Repeat that which makes you tingle with joy, smile contentedly, or relax and feel at peace with yourself (you will be at peace once you fill your life with these things). Give them your full attention, if only for an instant. Shift your focus. Make yourself notice excitement, curiosity, or bliss. Never mind the "I don't deserve it" mechanism you've adopted. Experiencing joy is your birthright, your nature. Deserving to live in love (and in tune) with yourself is a human construct. You do not *deserve* to be you. You are you.

Do you get it?

Yes? No?

Whatever the case, it's all right. You're searching. You're allowing the search. That's enough. Your soul will guide you back to your natural state the moment you move away from it. You don't need to do anything except allow. In our human existence, other people teach us how to become "people," and most of them do so from their own place of forgetfulness. So, in our journey to adapt to the human reality, rarely do we stay in our natural state. Instead, we slowly (or quickly, depending on the circumstances) move farther and farther away from it, hiding it deeper and deeper below the surface. We go digging for gold. Or relationships. Or big cars and luxurious homes. Or the sweet buzz from a glass of wine or two. Or gossip. Or food.

Don't get me wrong. There's nothing wrong with these things in and of themselves, but often, they become a substitute for the natural buzz of being us. However, you're here because you desire to search for your truth. You're acting upon the pull from your soul to "get it." You have the power to ignore those confused, misguided messages your wonderful mind keeps repeating in its effort to protect you from evil. Why on earth would you continue listening to a voice that keeps telling you that you're not worthy of feeling good? What nonsense. What Non-Sense! You can choose to feel good. Truly.

"I don't know how to do that," you say? Try it:

Exercise – Loosen the Knot – II

As you move through your days, practise being curious:

"Does this feel good to me? This? Or this…"

"No? Okay, how about this…"

"Ah, yes. I liked that. Let's have more of that."

That's what your inquisitive self sounds like as you go about your daily life, (re)discovering what makes you smile, laugh, and quiver with excitement. What makes your heart sing? If you don't know, you will. Take it from someone who's been there. Not long ago, joy wasn't even a distant memory to me. I knew only the occasional moment of pleasure and giggles. But true, heartfelt joy? It didn't apply to me. I had no idea how to find it. I didn't "get it." It had to be an illusion. It was something we all sought (*Why?* I wondered, not yet aware that it's part of our nature as unlimited souls), but I thought I'd never find.

Fortunately, my soul kept pulling at me, longing to restore me to my nature, and I started listening. I'm stubborn. Although there were long (and I mean loooooooong) moments where I couldn't feel the pull, I kept searching, wondering, asking. My soul, my listening, and my stubbornness have led me to this moment.

So there you have it. As the morning light brightens on the horizon, I sense the tiredness in my body. What I have just shared with you felt important; I couldn't leave it until later. I'd sooner sacrifice sleep than disturb this flow. I hope my words can help you find your own flow. Nothing would make me happier than if you found that tingle in your heart so you could unveil your colours, your natural beauty. Loosen your knot. Reawaken your essence. It's what you are.

It's time I go back to sleep.

June 4, at our kitchen table

My dearest Fredrik,

A new day has dawned. I'm back in our kitchen after having seen you off to school. Tired, but appreciative. However tired I might be, I love our mornings together. Waking you up with a cup of tea after my quiet morning routine, turning the radio on, letting classical music fill the house. Making your packed lunch, sitting at the breakfast table with you before you leave. You're lucky we live so close to your school. It gives you an easy start to your day. And I'm lucky I can choose to work at home. It means I'll be here to greet you when you return. For now.

We're managing well, my love, and I'm thankful for the time we spend together. We're comfortable and at ease with each other and respect each other's needs. I value our conversations—your wonderful sense of humour, your wise reflections, and your vast knowledge (already… sometimes, you stun me, Fredrik.) All these things have brought you through some of the most painful experiences a boy can have in his life: two of your best friends moving far away; your parents divorcing; moving house not once, but twice; losing our beloved dogs Juno and Lobo; and your dad's illness. Yes, I've been by your side, but you made it. You decided not to let fear rule your mind, or your life. You stepped out of the painful circle of anxiety and rose to the occasion, allowing your natural optimism and positive outlook on life to govern your days. I couldn't be prouder.

Yet, despite your awareness and strength, there's new wisdom for you to discover. There always is, and I might still have something to contribute to your growth. Not by changing your circumstances, lecturing you on how to handle strife, or trying to lift your burdens off your shoulders, but by loving you (as I continue to learn, heal, and grow myself), and by writing this testimony for you to turn to in your own time.

There are more exercises—experiences—I'd like to share. These practices might help you "loosen your knot" further and allow you to embrace your strength, wisdom, and flow even more. The exercises are powerful, though it might take a little practice to get the gist of them, and a pinch of curiosity and patience.…

Meditation – Lean into Your Higher Self

Relax. Lean into the unknown.

Trust. Lean into the future.

Lean into your energy, your "higher self"—the essence that surrounds you, permeates you, and is anchored within you.

Do all this with your imagination and with your body.

Explore.

I know what you're thinking. First you must figure out what your essence is, right? Not really. Pretend you've got it figured out, even if you don't understand what it entails. Imagine you're a sorcerer, a guru, or a Zen master. Whatever works for you. Then find it. Look for it. Ask yourself, as with "the eye of the Divine," *Where is it?*

Go for a walk or sit still. It doesn't matter. Search for the You that surrounds you, permeates you, radiates from you, and expresses your entire being. Search for the You that is of the Divine, the You that is your nature and your starting point in this life and beyond.

Meditation – Heal Yourself

Imagine a field of energy around you (there is one). Imagine you can sense, know, and see the colours in this field. You can pretend to see it from the outside, or from your perspective in the middle of it. It doesn't matter. Amuse yourself. Explore.

Imagine you can feel this energy, like a bubble surrounding you. Imagine you can stretch it (you can). Pull it in (you can). The intention is all you need. Don't worry about "getting it."

Now, imagine you can lean into it. Feel its support. Its warmth. Its protection. Its power.

Feel You. All of You. All. Of. You. Isn't it lush?

When you explore, does anything feel uncomfortable, dense, or "sticky?"

Some people perceive their energy as sticky, especially if it's packed with "un-truths." Pretend you're a magician. Magically, with a wand or with your bare hands, whizz away whatever's making you uncomfortable. Or shake

it off. Or imagine a large magnet outside your bubble, pulling out everything that isn't your energy, anything that doesn't feel light, open, or exciting. Anything that doesn't feel "you." (Are you experiencing goosebumps, shivers, nausea, or tears while doing this? Great. You're shifting your energy.)
Imagine.

Finally (and this you don't want to forget), imagine pulling in all the energy that is yours from wherever you left it: with other people (we do), in the past and the future (we certainly do that), in other events.

You've cleared your space—your bubble of energy—of that which isn't yours. Now you can fill it up with your own unique, vast Self. You can pull yourself together.

Imagine. Go with it. Pretend you're psychic. Become the psychic you truly are.

Now, lean into your field.

Can you sense the strength?

The support?

Congratulations. You've performed your first high-frequency self-healing. You loosened your knot (which is what healing is).
Remember. Always remember: You're an unlimited being anchored in a body. Your body expresses you. It's a powerful, beautiful manifestation of you in this world. It's time to embrace yourself, all of you—body, mind, soul.
You. Are. Beautiful.

A walk with Bella and a few reflections later, in the kitchen

I mentioned your body, didn't I?

There's more to say about this topic, of course. Especially in our time, when we subject our bodies to all kinds of misunderstandings and even abuse. Let me ask you: How long has it been since you cared for your body? I mean genuinely cared? Not pampered it, pushed it to its limit in a workout, stretched it to the unbearable in a yoga pose, or fed it nothing but nourishing and energizing food. I mean cared for it—from your heart? How long has it been since you loved your body for all it is—whatever shape or form, and however disturbed you may feel about it?

Yesterday? Last week? Last month? Last year? Last decade? Never, in your memory?

Whatever the case may be for you, most humans have never—past the first innocent stage of childhood (provided your earliest years were safe)—felt love, compassion, wonder, or care for their bodies. What a wild, absurd human construct. Why on earth should we not love our bodies?

For whatever reason, our societies, parents, peers, history, and religion teach us not to love our bodies (the Divine doesn't teach us this). As we grow up to become "responsible" adults and citizens of the world, we move away from our nature, that which embodies (so to speak) not only our soul and spirit but also our physical manifestation of our soul and spirit. Little by little, as we learn to be human beings, we succumb to the voices of those who have been here longer than us as the "Voices of Truth." Day by day, these Voices of Truth become our own voices—whispering at first, then developing into an impenetrable shout—and we move farther away from our natural selves. Until, if we're lucky (or we adhere to divine guidance or our fellow humans' guidance), we realise they aren't the Voices of Truth at all. Only by then, it's too late to (easily) retrieve our natural state of Being (or so we think). We fight. We fight ourselves and our nature. Sometimes we set off to fight the belief systems that have permeated our lives for so long. In our desperate search for a higher truth, we adopt other beliefs and stories to uncover that which our soul holds as our truth. We get stuck in new patterns and ideas—ideas we adopt from people who themselves have been looking for a way out of the illusions—the untruths, if you wish—and who experience that they've found the Truth. They've "seen the light." Until we recognise they aren't the "Voices of Truth," either. The light they've seen might be their light, but it's not necessarily ours. Thus, the saga continues.

Unless we stop.

And listen.

And investigate in wonder, searching for our own Voice of Truth.

Our Voice. Our Truth.

Whatever that may be.

Remember those sci-fi films and series where someone gets teleported from one place to another? My generation might remember it from *Star Trek* or other such "old" series (which have become trendy again. Hey!).[5] You might know it from somewhere else. I'm referring to when the character's physical body breaks up and fades out as they are beamed out of their present location and become a physical being in a new location. I'm talking about the moment of transition from the physical to energy—and back again.

Now, imagine this is an image of you. Not because you're being teleported from one place to another (Wouldn't that be fun? Who knows—maybe we'll get there sometime, when we have evolved and learnt to master the energies), but because all the phases depicted in those films would be an image of your whole self at any one moment. Yes, you are a physical manifestation—a "knot," if you like—but you are also all the nuances of energy density moving through and expanding beyond your physical form. You're a dense, physical body with all the interesting sensations that come with the physical "dimension," and you're the field of energy permeating and surrounding your body.

Do you know that—with practice—you can see this energy with your own eyes?

Let's try it. Let's have some fun:

---

⁵ I'm referring to the original *Star Trek* TV series created by Gene Roddenberry.

Exercise – "See" Your Energy Field

Stand in front of a mirror—preferably with a light, plain background behind you.

Focus your gaze at the outline of your physical body.

"Un-focus" your gaze (the way you do when you're daydreaming or thinking about something other than the present moment—when you're "far away"), all the while keeping your gaze on the edge of your body.

Notice any hint of light that surrounds your physical being—like a lighter hue of the background. It might be just a hint at first—a thin line of light as you first notice the densest part of your energy field—but if you keep looking, you might notice that it expands. (It's a bit like staring at a stereogram with a hidden 3D image. You prepare your brain to "see" and grasp the image and stare with unfocused eyes until the image "comes out" of the background.)

Can you see it? Play with it. Be curious (always), explore (always), and have fun (always).

You can take it a step farther. You can look around and see the energies surrounding the trees and mountains, or other people:

Exercise – "See" Energy Fields Around You

For this exercise, be mindful that you don't stare at someone you don't know—you don't want to be invasive. I find staring at animals can be a little tricky too, as they're aware of your gaze and often move away if they find it too imposing or threatening. Try for yourself and see how it works for you.

Start by using the same technique as in the previous example to see the energy radiating from a tree, for instance. Or the light surrounding a loved one who has agreed to being gazed at. You might even try it on a person standing on a stage (they're there to be seen anyway), or a group of people gathered together.

Try this against different backgrounds: the blue sky, a wall, a plain backdrop on a stage. With practice, you might see different colours in the energy field. That's when it gets interesting and fun.

(Again: please be mindful you're not invading anyone's privacy. Don't try to interpret what you see—you'd be "looking into" someone's personal sphere. You can do that if you've trained as a healer and have learnt to distinguish and understand our energetic boundaries, and to set your human perspectives and judgments aside. Until then, I implore you to just observe as an exercise to expand and increase your awareness.)

Just like in *Star Trek*, where Scotty "beams up" Captain Kirk by dematerializing him in one location and rematerializing him in a new location seamlessly, there are no borders between the energies we express through our bodies and our soul's higher vibration radiating outwards, beyond our bodies. Let me elaborate (I know this is a tricky concept to grasp):

We have established that we are energy, and that energy moves even in the densest form. Our soul is energy, and it flows through all aspects of us. It's the vibration that surrounds our bodies (like a luminous cloud following us everywhere), and it's the vibration we've gathered *in* our bodies. Most of us have densified this physical energy by stuffing our fears and heavy emotions into our bodies (like tightening the knot). But it's still our energy. (We sometimes take on other people's energies. Becoming familiar with your unique vibration is a great way to discern and release that which is not yours.)

In other words, there's no either/or to what we are. There's no border between our souls and our bodies—our expressions include all. As it "beams" into a visible form, the closer this soul energy gets to the body, the denser, more visible, and more tactile it becomes. We're all at once: denser energies manifested through our physical presence and lighter energies moving beyond our bodies out into the universe. Our soul expresses itself in, through, and beyond our bodies, just like the silk scarf. We vibrate our timbre, colour, and light not only through our physical embodiment but also through our free-flowing soul as it dances among the stars. (Yup. We can do that, too. Imagine that.) Hence, we not only experience life on earth through our physical senses; we can also sense the energies surrounding us, and we can expand our energy as far out as we wish.

Science acknowledges today that energy radiates out beyond our visible, physical selves, as well as moving through our bodies—all in one big, magnificent Whole. How does this help us? By reminding us of the flow that is ours naturally, and by guiding us to loosen the densified knots in our bodies so our healing can begin and the soul restore itself.

You might have to embrace the idea of having a soul. You might have to buy into the concept that energy is part of your expression, that there's more to you than meets the eye, and that you are, in fact, larger than life. Even if you're not ready to go there, you can still have fun with this. Try it out:

Meditation – Discover Your Truth

> Taste the flavour of this statement: "I am larger than life."
>
> "How do I taste a statement?" you ask.
>
> Repeat "I am larger than life" to yourself—silently or out loud (or both)—and observe the sensations. How does the statement resonate in your body, your emotions, or your mind? Do any images come to you? Any sounds, smells, or ideas? Does the flavour, the experience of the statement, feel familiar? Or does it feel unfamiliar—like a foreign language? Do you reject it with every fibre of your being, or does it awaken your curiosity? Does it make you angry, or does the idea excite you?
>
> Observe your emotions and determine if the belief inherent in the statement is part of your truth: The lighter, the closer to your truth. It's all good. It's yours to unravel in your own way.

If the flavour doesn't appeal to you, it's okay. It's up to you what belief system you adopt. In my experience, we're greater than life. Anything else makes little sense to me anymore.

But I digress. My point is (and this can change your reality once you absorb it) that your body is not a vessel for your soul and spirit. Your body is an anchor for your extended vibration— your energy and light. At the same time, it embodies your energy and light. It's the "knot" that lets you walk on the earth whilst your greater self moves and dances around you.

"Then why," you might ask, "is it causing me so much pain? Why all this illness? This stiffness? Why do we age?" There are many fascinating ideas about the reason for our illnesses and pain. I've investigated several of them—sometimes in depth by following programmes offered both live and online,[6] sometimes briefly (because it didn't resonate at the time), and sometimes by reading inspirational books. Some teachings stay with me. Some don't. Some I have expanded on. Some I have discarded as I came closer to my truth. I am, however, confident about this: *I am a soul.* I'm also my body. My essence, my soul, my Being—in short, my energy—infuses every cell in my body. Every cell in my body will radiate the love I am the moment I let it.

How does that work?

Well, if you're a soul with an essence, and this essence is Love (because we are of the Divine), and you're also your physical body, then your body should be Love, too. Right? Indulge me— I'm trying to express something important, and I need a little help from above to clarify my words.

A moment later, after a brief meditation – back at our kitchen table

Imagine holding a baby: soft, tender, dependent, open, curious. The baby fixes its gaze on you—big, blue eyes, wide open with wonder, though unable to focus for long. It reaches out its hand, touches your skin. Your heart melts. For a moment, you're nothing but pure Love. Your soul reaches out and embraces this vulnerable little creature. Your body softens. You're one with the gentle care you feel for this baby. You're one with the unconditional Love you (for once) have allowed to flow through you. All you can sense in the moment is the connection to this pure representation of Love.

---

[6] *Astarte/Soulspring* by Princess Märtha Louise and Elisabeth Nordeng; *ThetaHealing* with Anett Wang; *Unlimited Abundance* with Christie Marie Sheldon (online); *Past Life Regression* with Marije Terluin (online); *Transforming Your Life Through Near-Death Experiences* with Anita Moorjani (online); *Quantum Jumping* with Burt Goldman (online); *Cultivating Intuition & A Balanced Mind* with Jeffrey Allen; *The Art of Manifesting* with Regan Hillyer; *The Champion Mindset* with Florencia Andrés; *Leveraging the Universe* by Mike Dooley (book); *The Power of Now* by Eckhart Tolle (book); and individual readings with trained, professional intuitive readers and healers as well as personal meditation and self-readings.

Can you feel (in this moment) every cell of your body vibrating with this Love? This is what I was referring to when I asked, "How long has it been since you cared for your body?"

When was the last time you felt your body in unison with your spirit, and your soul? How long since you loved your entire being in this way? A long time, right? Can you imagine how great it would be to be you if you could move through your day loving and caring for your body in this way? You just have to imagine a moment of pure Love, and you're there. Boom! Never mind the stress and pressure of working out, eating right, stretching, breathing, building muscle, and putting all those beauty products on it (okay, all this can be delicious, too). That's all good, but we want to move away from the stress and fear of not getting it "right." The moment you care for your body the way you would care for that baby, that's when you start to heal and thrive and dance and laugh. That's when you choose to eat a delicious salad, push your body to the limit in a workout, or stretch and breathe in a yoga class because it feels good. It feels natural, uplifting, exciting. That's when you pamper yourself with delightful, luxurious treatments because you want to in the moment.

Doesn't it sound easy? And fun? Doesn't it make sense? But how do you do this? If you take time to explore these ideas on your daily walks, or on your way to school or work—or wherever you're on your way to—you might find an answer within yourself. In the meantime, I'll continue sharing what I sense, understand, and experience. Maybe my words will ignite a memory somewhere deep in your soul.

Oh, by the way… My story is only another story. It's a story about how the veil was lifted from my eyes (and believe me, it was heavy. My relationship to my body was at best hate-full and tense). My story is about how I loosened my knot, opened to my flow, and came closer to healing. I hope my story ignites your curiosity enough that you (knowingly or not) follow your soul's tune.

Does my story motivate you to investigate, listen, or wonder at your own images? Wonderful. Will you lift your gaze (inner, outer, or both?) and look around you until you recognise that which strikes a chord in you? Marvellous. Do my words remind you to listen to the whispers of your soul, to sound your own tone, or to seek your unique expression? If so, I will have fulfilled my purpose. I could wish for no more.

I'll be back soon. I'm enjoying sharing all these ideas and experiences with you.

*June 6, the day before my birthday, on our terrace
overlooking the garden and the glorious oak tree*

(A perfect day for the Big Question)

So, why are we here?
Yes. Let's not shy away. Let's ask the Big Question and explore.
Because to be honest, *I don't know.*
Do you?
Does anyone?
I don't think so.
Why?
Because we're human beings.

Being human involves manoeuvring in a dense territory energy-wise, which, as we've already discussed, makes it tricky to flow in a natural way as a soul. We've adopted all kinds of strange mechanisms in our attempt to make sense of who we are and why we're here. If we want to "come home" to ourselves, we must release these mechanisms. In our present lifespan, we sometimes lose the struggle.
But…
We can still wonder. Reflect.
We can still heal, rise, and remember who we are. What we are.
We can still remember Love. And freedom.

Beloved Fredrik,

Have I told you how happy I am that you're here? I am. Sincerely. I feel it in every cell of my body, although at present, I don't know when you'll be reading this. I might even be "dead." But still... I feel you. I feel you in my heart and in my life. You've touched me like no other human being has, and across all time and space, I hold an immense love for you. I sense your passion, beauty, strength, and presence. I'm so, so happy you came into my life. It's delightful that you're hanging on and allowing me to ramble on with my perspectives and reflections, here, and in our life together.

I wonder: Are you any wiser yet? Does any of this make sense? Only you can say. All I can do is trust the task I've embraced, guiding you to the best of my ability.

Now, let me get back to the big question: *Why are we here?*

I can't be sure. I can imagine, believe, and consider, but I cannot know for certain. However, let me share what I experienced in this morning's meditation as I asked myself that same question. I'll try to translate my experience into words. (It takes courage, though. The words cannot reveal the wisdom, and I realise you might misunderstand them. I'll do my best).

We're not here for a reason at all!

I had to leave a little space there, to let the (shock)wave settle....

It was a delightful revelation—almost a relief—when it dawned on me. We don't have to make sense of our lives. We don't have to accomplish, learn, grow, become better people— none of that. We only have to *be*. Meaning we can be whoever we are, in energy, spirit, and body. We can:
Build.
Create.
Dream.

Explore.
Feel.
Grow.
Imagine.
Investigate.
Love.
Play.
Ponder.
Sing.
Sleep.
Speak.
Wonder.
Write….

All those magnificent things.
We can be all that—and more—because we can.

Let's use our imagination. Let's explore a probable scenario. Although first, I must remind you of the power of your imagination, the superpower we all possess as children but often lose sight of as we grow up and learn to be "rational" (again— what a wild human construct).

Your imagination is a powerful, beautiful tool for reconnecting to your essence and truth (and I mean "truth" in the sense of "what resonates with your unique essence"). It can help you explore and build an exciting, joyful life. Your imagination is part of your creative force. It's what moves you forward and through your life. Never underestimate it. Bring it into your life and make it as natural as breathing.

So, let's imagine…

You're a free soul, moving, dancing through the Universe. There's nothing holding you back. You're in the flow. You're connected to the Source of all Creation through your essence (some people call it God, the Creator, Allah, Jahve, or the Divine. I'm going to stick with the "Source" of Creation). You are what you are—a unique aspect of all Creation—though in this image you're not giving that connection (or your nature) a second thought. You Are. You're pure energy, playing with all the other energies around you. With some of them, you vibrate in unison. Some push your energy around. Some are of similar colours. But you're all connected to Source, to the Divine. You're all Love.

You gather with a group of fellow souls and discuss a possible new adventure. How about popping down to the blue planet— the blue pearl of the Universe—and exploring some of those sensations again? Smelling, tasting, touching, listening… and the emotions. Oh, my goodness, those emotions. They're tricky. Exciting too, though. There's trouble down there, apparently. Maybe you could unravel a few of those tight, hard knots down there so the souls get to dance again? There's an opening right now. You're close to some souls down there. Do you wish to join them again? Interact with them? Maybe loosen the knots you got tangled in together the last time you were there? Are you ready for the thrill—and the challenges—of the experience? It will differ from last time; it might even be a little tougher in certain areas. But there's potential for genuine excitement, too. You notice that more humans are reconnecting to their souls, to Love. How fun. They're starting to "get it." You recognise this as a great opportunity for you to lift some vibrations. You "look" around (you sense the energies around you and send your intention out to them) and ask, "Who has my back if I go? I need a team of energies to support me and guide me if I forget my way and lose sight of myself. A big team—eight would be great. Then I can be certain not to get lost. The last time (phew!), I was in the dark most of the time. That was a tough ride, let me tell you. Can we keep a clearer communication this time? Give me a big shout if you see me losing my way. Okay? This time, I'm going to investigate how to break through those weird barriers we—as human beings—keep putting around ourselves. It's as if we forget our bodies are energy too, and how our intentions and emotions impact everything we do and create. As crazy as it sounds, it's as if we forget what Love is!

"Wouldn't it be great," you think, "if I could remember this when I'm there and help more humans remember, too? What if we could all see and comprehend how beautiful it is—Earth, heaven, and all—no matter what shape or form we're in? I suppose that's going to be my goal. Yes. That will be my goal."

"Which of my colours do I need to enhance in my human presence to manage that goal?" you might wonder. "Purple?" you say. "Ah, yes, of course. To match the physical body's higher energy centre—the crown, that which allows me to connect to divine wisdom and guidance in a better way, and to 'see' the other souls. And green? Yes, the heart. I must emphasise the heart this time, to bring on that 'lovin' feeling' (I seem to remember those words in a song from last time I was there—am I right?). Yes? Awesome. So, where's that opening? I see it. Wish me luck!"

And off you go…

To inspect. Sense. Play. Help some. Heal some. To find the opening, the energies, that will make it easier for you and other people to remember who they are and simply *be*.

A fun idea, isn't it?

Is it true? I don't know, but there's something there. It's something to wonder about and with which to amuse yourself. It won't harm you to contemplate it. The idea might even help you understand how your team of energies and guides (I believe we each have a team with us) can support you. You ask for their help. It's as simple as that.

What we do know is this: We are Love. Love is the essence of All That Is. It's our natural state. Love is joy, contentment, laughter, gratitude, ease, and all those things that remind us in our everyday lives (consciously or not) that we are Love. Because when we engage in those delights, we forget how we sometimes believe that we're not Love.

Think about it: Regardless of how lost we feel, we all keep looking for Love. We search in the most interesting places for this state of being because we keep longing for our nature. We long to regain our flow, colours, and natural vibration. We do so because when we're in our natural state, we're in balance, and balance is what the Universe seeks to regain: equilibrium, peace, and unity.

If we're too far removed from our natural state of Love, we might engage in nasty or harmful actions. Anything to experience connection and significance (two beautiful expressions of Love) and remember the sense of Love we have hidden somewhere deep in our hearts and souls.

But when we're connected to ourselves and each other through love? Ah…. we breathe easier, smile more, relax, and burst into song! We flow. There's no resistance. It's pure essence. Pure truth.

I could go on about this, but I won't. I'll leave it up to your magnificent soul, which has made the choice of diving into this roller-coaster of a life to see what it's like. You know this. You do. Your soul does. And your mind, your beautiful mind, works hard to show you what it understands—from lived experience. Your mind is powerful. It's unstoppable once it gets going. What an amazing tool!

Hence, my next question: How long has it been since you cared for your mind?

Hmmm. Good question, right? Especially if you're on this spiritual path of trying to get behind and beyond your so-called disruptive mind. It's amazing how, when seeking guidance on our spiritual path, people—teachers, healers, and mentors alike—tell us our minds are wrong. Again, notice the inclination to disregard a part of ourselves. Notice how we make our physical representation of our divine selves wrong. Why do we keep doing that?

Your mind is a part of you in the same way your body is. They're both aspects of you. Love them. Care for them. The power your mind holds is immense, and it's convinced the unlimited, radiant you that you are limited, dumb, and worthless. With such power available to you, don't you want to be friends with it? Don't you want to embrace it, and teach it the truth, so it can free itself and show you how to soar, flow, rise?

Go on… give your mind a big hug. (In your imagination, of course, but you can use your hands to aid you, the way you hold your hands on your chest to bring your attention to your heart.) In fact, the last thing I'm going to share with you today is this:

Exercise – Embrace Your Whole Self

Imagine giving your body a Big Hug.[7]

Then give your Mind one.

Then your Soul. (Don't ask me how—try it out. You'll find a way).

Then—give your entire self one massive, big embrace.

Stop reading. Do it now. Embrace yourself with all the love you can muster. Then add more. Don't worry if you can't remember what love is. (I didn't for the longest time.) Pretend. Your soul will do the rest. It has your back. It will never let you down. It will never, ever fail you. How could it? It. Is. Love.

My dearest Fredrik,

I'm grateful and filled with love at the thought that you might be drinking in these words. Even if you're not reading this, I'm grateful because you're You. Thank you. I couldn't wish for a more beautiful birthday present: imagining you reading this book sometime in the future. Imagining how my experiences and remembrance of who I am—who we are—might give you what you're looking for in your healing journey.

---

[7] You can try the Butterfly Hug, which can be found on YouTube. I like the video on the TYF Support Group's channel.

June 7, on our terrace in the early morning sun—it's my birthday!

Good morning, my darling.

I woke up with a smile this morning, as I knew I would. It's a beautiful day. I saw the blue sky through the skylight above my head and felt blessed. Then a horrifying thought hit me: What if the idea of there not being any meaning to our existence deflated or confused you and caused you to lose hope? *It would negate everything I'm working to do. Please don't despair. There's hope. There's meaning. There's meaning in* being. *That's enough. At the core of the non-meaning I was laying before you yesterday is the one thing that has meaning: Love. "All You Need Is Love,"*[8] *as they say (or sing). Yes. The meaning lies in Love. It lies in* being *Love. It's what we come from. It's who we are. Even Mother Earth is Love. Creation. She too is a physical manifestation of her large, powerful, creative, Divine essence. Just as we are. You (body, mind, soul), Mother Earth (the Blue Pearl of the Universe), Life, and Creation—we're all connected to this one magnificent state of Being: Love. How can there*

---

[8] The Beatles, "All You Need Is Love," Composers & Lyrics: John Lennon and Paul McCartney, Producer: George Martin, recorded at EMI studios, London, 1967.

not be meaning in that? Think about it. In the moments
you feel joy, happiness, or peace, do you need to search for
meaning? I rest my case. Now, move on through your day
with excitement and contentment. It's all you have to do,
my love. All you need to know.

We are Love, then....

This knowledge is ancient, of course, but (as we wake up to the old sensation) it's also new. More than ever before, people are searching to reconnect to Love. As we do so, our reconnection differs from the past. We've moved through some heavy, challenging imbalances and dark shadows in the history of our world, and the Love we're reconnecting to has always been there, at the core of our existence, confirming itself and becoming more prevalent than ever before as we continue to reunite with it and nourish it. That's where the hope lies. All We Need Is Love. When we're living Love (no, I'm not talking about romantic love between two people, exhilarating and beautiful though it may be—that's a different story), that's all that matters.

Let's look at Mother Earth. Try to imagine sending a heartbeat, or a thought, to the centre of the earth. Use that superpower of yours (remember your imagination). Imagine what her centre, her energy feels like. Imagine she has a pulsating heart which pours out this energy to all she's creating—all the beauty and power that we encounter throughout our lives here, with her. Can you recognise the Love? To me, the heartbeat of Mother Earth is a pure, mother-like love. She's strong, dynamic, and gentle. All the beauty we see around us are the miracles of her physical manifestation. Connecting to her in this way is a beautiful way to ground yourself, too. I'll show you how in a minute.

What I'm saying is this: all we have to do (the only thing that makes sense) to find the place where *being* is enough is to find those lush, beautiful sensations inside ourselves that resonate with our essence of Love. After all, these good sensations are what we seek every day, whether through physical stimulants (such as delicious chocolate or a big, warm embrace), or in our deep soul-searching quests. Mother Earth can help us with this discovery. In our earthly presence we are blessed not only with the spiritual forces that reflect our higher selves (once we remember to listen) but also with the grounded, all-powerful forces of Love and Creation emanating from Her to which our bodies one day "shall return." Unconditional Love is available to us both from above and below. If we remember to open to it and if we dare to receive it.

Let's try a short meditation. You can do this wherever you are—it only requires a few moments of focus, and once you've practised it, you can do it even with your eyes open:

Meditation – Connect Above and Below

Close your eyes. Take a deep breath. Observe your feet on the ground. Bring your attention to the top of your head. Next, bring your focus to your heart centre. For extra focus, put your hands on your chest. Now, imagine sending a heartbeat out through the crown of your head to the centre of the Universe. Don't worry about "knowing" where this centre is—imagine you can sense it. Imagine, as your heartbeat reaches the heart of the Universe (some people call it "God"), that the Universe—in pure joy at reconnecting to your beautiful essence—meets your heartbeat, and in return pours a beautiful shower of light down to you.

Imagine this light pouring down through the top of your head, through your head, neck, spine, shoulders, arms, chest and heart, tummy, hips, legs, feet, and all the way into the ground. "Watch" as this light (the energy) continues down, all the way into the centre, the heart, of Mother Earth. Again, acknowledge the beauty of Her motherly love as She rejoices at the connection and sends all Her beautiful love back up to you: through your feet, legs, hips, tummy, chest and heart, arms, shoulders, spine, neck, head, and out through the top of your head.

Receive the Love and support from above and below. Welcome it. Allow your heart to remember what it's like to be loved. And to love.

Imagine your heart, touched by Universal and Earthly Love, opens a golden casket within, revealing the core—the golden drop, or crystal, or sparkle—of your essence. Your Love. Imagine you can allow this speck of Love to expand, radiating out like a big sun from the centre of your being. Allow it to grow, expand farther, ignited by the beauty and power from above and below. Let it radiate through your whole body. Let it emanate beyond your body, until the Love from your heart, the Universe, and the Earth permeate and surround you.

Take a deep breath of gratitude. Set the intention to allow your heart to shine and support you for the rest of your day.

Open your eyes. Smile.

Now let's look at how you can discover that which can bring you to a place of joy, peace, and excitement in your everyday life. How can you enhance your sense of well-being and connection where you are today? By exploring what makes you feel *good*. I don't mean the escape that comes with drugging yourself or hiding in a TV series for hours on end (which can be fun too), but whatever makes you feel good in your core. It can be small or large things, events, nature, or people. It doesn't matter. Only you can know what brings you to a state of joy, excitement, or contentment. Write these things down. Put a note on your fridge, next to the mirror in your bathroom, or on the wall by your bed so the list is the first thing you see each morning. As you discover more things, add them to the list. As I noted earlier, the moment you become aware of a bounce in your step, notice your tension and pain melting away, or find yourself singing along with the songs on the radio—that's when you're connected! That's when you've shifted your focus. That's when you've filled your life with uplifting experiences rather than those that bring you down. That's when your life has taken a turn towards Being in Love with yourself and with your life.

I believe our purpose lies in reminding ourselves and others that we are this Love, this essence. (Remember the imagined dialogue "you" had with your guides before descending to the earth? How you hoped to help people remember the Love? Like that.) Can you imagine what would happen to a child if her parents supported and encouraged her when she expressed delight and joy, rather than only when she voiced frustration or pain? Of course, we as parents want to help our children when they're in need, but if a child gets encouragement and support when she's happy, wouldn't that teach her that happiness and love is what she's all about? Wouldn't it teach her to keep doing whatever she needs to do to stay happy and in love? Unfortunately, most of us haven't received this type of guidance in our lives, as our world has been off track for generations. We've been told not to shout, not to laugh, not to make too much noise, and not to talk so much. It's no wonder we have so many demons and disruptive patterns to heal from.

I witnessed this yesterday in a store. A little girl, around three years old, was chatting away, excited and curious, asking one question after another. She was unstoppable, and we know how annoying that can be when we're trying to get things done. This was the case with the little girl's father. "Do you have to talk *all the time?*" he burst out. The girl continued, though, oblivious to the father's stern voice. He tried to milden his tone by hunching down, meeting her eyes, and "jokingly" saying to her: "You talk a lot, don't you?" She stopped, with a puzzled expression on her little face, as if to say: "Did I get it wrong again? Is this happy feeling leading me into trouble—again?"

The last part was in my imagination, of course. I didn't stop to study her expression. But it's the message our children get when we stop them from expressing their pure excitement. What we're doing is telling them that being in love with life itself is wrong. It's no wonder we stop ourselves from being happy. We've learnt it's wrong. We've learnt that joyful expressions are noisy, disturbing, and annoying. (Expressing frustration and anger are too, of course, but at least they give us the attention we're looking for.)

Until now.

Because today and for the rest of your life, you have permission to be happy. Today is the day you remind yourself of what joy feels like. You can be curious. You can practise by bringing into your life that which makes you feel good. Do it now. Then do it again tomorrow. And the day after that. Notice the tingling sensations of joy, contentment, and happiness in your tummy, heart, and mind every time they appear. Let the warm, peaceful sensations lead the way. Receive them. Indulge. Give thanks. Don't be afraid to put yourself first. It's not selfish. It's your obligation. Your responsibility. When you put yourself first, you put Creation first. After all, you're an aspect of Creation, remember? When you neglect yourself, you neglect Creation. That's how powerful you are.

If you need a reason to take care of yourself and teach yourself that you're allowed to be happy, that, in fact, it's key to your existence (and it's what we all are), remind yourself of this responsibility. Do so until you don't need a reason because you own the truth—you can be happy, because you *are*. Happiness is peace and Love. It's the meaning of All That Is. Go find it. Be it.

Whether you know how to come back to the state of Love or you don't makes no difference. Your permission to be happy will always be there for you to embrace when you're ready.

It's nature. Keep searching, listening, investigating. "Where is happiness? Where is this essence of Love which is supposed to be me? Is it in my heart? In my spine? In my energy? Is it around the next corner? What does it feel like, I wonder?" Keep asking those questions like the child you once were—until you get it. (Remember my ear-moving experience? And my search to see myself with the eye of the Divine?) You might get it in a flash at first, then in glimpses. Eventually, you'll acknowledge it as your natural state. Not all the time (please don't expect that). As human beings, battling with obstacles appears to be part of our reality no matter what. But you'll recognise the state of ease and contentment as the foundation of your existence, the pillar upon which you stand, regardless of what happens. You'll understand how to return to it every time you lose sight of it because now you have a clear map of where it is. You can always find it. You can always—*always*—find your place of peace, joy, love.

Sound good?

Meditation helps, by the way.

See you soon!

Much, much love.

My love,

What a gorgeous day yesterday turned out to be. Thank you for joining in my little birthday celebration. It was all I could have wished for: you, a couple of close friends, beautiful weather, a swim in the sea, a delicious meal, and some good, warm embraces. I never used to enjoy my birthday. I found it too difficult to receive back then. But now I can indulge in the beautiful sensation that receiving is. Because I can, and because I'm blessed: I'm blessed with gifts, friendship, love, and for all that I give thanks. Did you know some people say gratitude is the fuel of abundance and happiness? "Great fuel," I heard someone say once. It's easy to look at gratitude as a tool to achieve grander things, but when you're grateful, I'm sure you can agree the feeling itself is abundance. And happiness. Gratitude uplifts you and enhances your life in every way. Remember that, my love, and you will have a happy life.

"What about being of service?" you ask. "What about other people? Isn't helping others what we're here for? We can't just go around feeling good on our own!" Let me answer those questions from my perspective. (Remember—you must choose your own perspective.)

If you desire to be of service, then be of service. Why not? But be of service to yourself as well. When you feel a tingling joy in your heart at the notion of helping someone, do it. If you feel a lush, warm feeling at the idea of giving something of beauty to someone, then please do. When you smile at the thought of doing that one thing someone has asked for, go do it. All I wish for is that you (and I, and all of us) realise the power and beauty in doing the same for ourselves, and the responsibility we have to do so. First. Or at least at the same time. Where do you suppose those excited sensations, delightful feelings, and smiles come from? From your natural source of Love. It makes sense, doesn't it?

Again, I'm not here to tell you how to live your life. Yet, I keep holding the hope in my heart that you'll find a spark from reading my words that reminds you to rediscover who you are, and value this You. Someone once said that if everyone were kind to themselves, we wouldn't have to worry about being kind to others. We'd all be kind naturally. Why? Because we'd have "got it!" We'd have convinced ourselves in our hearts that we come from Love, that we are Love, and hence we are worthy of kindness. We'd be able to live it. We'd have peace.

But until then, we can move through our days in curiosity and wonder. (Am I repeating myself? I should hope so.) *What's this emotion telling me? Why am I repeating this pattern? Where am I trying to go with this thought?* And, the magical question, the vital one in our search for light, peace, and enlightenment is: *Where can I find joy?*

I believe we're all on our path to rediscover our nature, the truth, and Love. It seems inconceivable when we look around us, when the news keeps invading our homes with images of the pain people are living in certain parts of our world. I understand. Nevertheless, I continue to believe it. There are countless people already on the path—more than ever—and the young generation is benefitting from this. A beautiful, strong, vibrant young generation is emerging in these times....

My beloved,

Are you aware of your soul's strong intention of staying in alignment with who you are—the intention you carried with you when joining us "down here"? Do you understand the strength of your soul and its dedication to lift our world to a higher place? Yes, the awakening and the healing we, your parents' generation, are undergoing is important. It enables you and your peers to integrate all that you are in a better way than we could. We can lay the groundwork, but you will shift it. You and your children. Granted, it might take a generation or two before we're there, but you'll make it. I know it in my heart, and this book is my humble contribution to the groundwork. It's exciting, don't you agree? A bit daunting, perhaps? Have no fear. It's who you are, and you're not alone.

Have you ever heard of "the hundredth monkey effect"? The term is based on work by a group of Japanese researchers in the 1950s.[9] The researchers decided to teach a new behaviour to a small group of monkeys on an island. As their work progressed, they discovered that monkeys across the sea and on different islands picked up the same behaviour—without the groups having been in direct communication with one another. The shift happened when one hundred monkeys (or thereabouts) on the first island had picked up the skill.

Other scientists, of course, have contested this. In our world, someone will usually challenge what appears to be "magic." But like I said before, I believe in magic. Don't you? Let's follow the

---

[9] Koshima research popularized by Lyall Watson, *Lifetide: The Biology of the Unconscious*, 1979.

theory a little further. What if, once a large enough group of monkeys (read: people) have learnt a skill (in our case: being kind to ourselves), the energy of the skill becomes so potent it can ripple through the air, like concentric circles in water, to people beyond our immediate surroundings. (Note that this "energy ripple" of kindness comes in addition to all those wonderful smiles, hugs, and words of encouragement you share with your loved ones, and all the inspiring stories on the internet anyone can read anywhere in the world.) I trust we're heading towards a more balanced, loving world—a Utopia, if you like.

"What about the people who are living through wars, pandemics, and destructive conditions?" Let me remind you of this: we can always send healing energies of love and hope, and do our best to stop the atrocities, no matter where we are. However, we can never accumulate enough pain in our own lives to ease theirs. So don't. All it will do is add to and intensify those devastating energies in the Whole. Increase the love instead. Be Love. Be the centre of your concentric circles and let those good vibrations do the work.

Wouldn't it be great if, a few generations down the line, people picked up this book and smiled, saying: "Look at this! She's talking about those wars and fears that used to run this world. I'd forgotten how that was the reality of our ancestors. How curious. She was right, though. We made it."

Wouldn't it be wonderful?

Let me return to the concept of being of service to yourself, and to the idea of being of service to others when it feels good. I'll share a story with you. It's how I "got it" for the first time.

When I was in "training" at Astarte (later Soulspring)[10] to re-learn how to open to Source and Love, and to my light,

---

[10] Astarte/Soulspring school for personal growth in Oslo closed in 2017 when the owners, Elisabeth Nordeng and Princess Märtha Louise decided to go separate ways. I attended the school from 2012 – 2015.

healing skills, and clear vision (yes, I have that too, more so as I keep looking, asking, wondering), we sometimes invited people in to receive a practice healing. It was a beautiful way to enhance our abilities while allowing people an opportunity to receive. This story is about one of those practice sessions, only this time there weren't enough people for us all to work with. I asked if I could "hold" the energy for all the others instead. "Holding the energy" means holding the intention of a high vibration and support for all the healing, and the people involved in the healing. (You try to sense the energy with your hands and "hold" it up or "send" uplifting light and energy into the room, intending to give the healers extra support. You create an energetic room in the room, so to speak.)

My mentors agreed, and I set about the task. I walked around the room, holding the energy for all the healers and their work. After a while, I had to stop and sit down. My back was killing me with pain. It was way too heavy for me. I had failed. I sat there, wondering what to do next. Then I remembered what our teachers kept repeating: "Give to yourself. Always give to yourself when you're doing any form of healing work." I hadn't figured out what that meant yet, let alone how to do it. But… As I sat there, thinking I was no good at this (the old story), repeating to myself I had no abilities and was not a spiritual person, convincing myself I was a fraud (my old demons had a go at me), I realised I had forgotten myself. I had tried supporting and holding everyone else in a high vibration, but who was supporting me? It was as if I had tried to hold the entire earth in my two hands, forgetting that I too was on the earth.

I stood up and tried again—this time including myself in the energy. Lo and behold, my back pain was gone. It was like magic. (Which it was, of course. Working with shifting, uplifting energy is magic. Try it. It starts with an intention. That's all you need.) When I told everyone afterwards about my experience, one instructor said, "That's why the energy shifted!" She'd felt it. They all had.

This. Is. The. Power. Of. Including. Yourself.

It's the power and beauty of caring for yourself first, while you're caring for someone else. You become strong, open, and free, and you can access the tingling joy in your heart that tells you that you're in alignment. You've remembered who you are. You've come Home.

I'll leave you with that for now. I have a client in a few minutes. Don't worry—I'll remember to include myself as I work to help her heal. One of the perks of writing this is that I keep getting reminded of the magic of being... well, magical.

Many blessings to you, from the blissful joy in my heart.

Today I had a revelation.

Have you noticed that often, the greatest revelations come when you're in a struggle, seeking to understand, "Why is this happening to me?" The seeking is key. If you keep seeking and asking questions, the chances of revelations landing in your conscious awareness are greater. So too for me today.

I was feeling vulnerable. I've been conducting a course, guiding people to open up and tap into their inner wisdom and higher self—and to the magic and all those beautiful energies out there we can work with and ask for help (our teams, remember?).

One participant was having so many amazing revelations, I could only marvel at her progress. She told me she meditates regularly and follows my guidance. Her dedication and openness reward her with powerful visions and healing. Witnessing her progress made me happy, and I'm thankful for being allowed to guide her to her path when she doesn't see it herself. But yesterday, after our session, I felt left out. It was as if she had access to experiences and wisdom I was missing. Earlier in the day, I'd come up against a challenge I haven't shaken off in my life yet, and it had left me feeling vulnerable. Now my teachings seemed beneficial to everyone but me. The old idea of not "getting it" invaded my mind, and I sulked like a child.

It was only for a moment, though. That old pattern doesn't have a hold on me anymore, thank goodness (and thanks to my healing journey). So you see, it's worth the effort: never give up. I looked closer, and the answer was staring me right in the face: The reason she was getting all those answers, revelations, and miraculous experiences was because she sat down, asked questions, and listened.

Ha!

This is what I do for all my clients, but how long has it been since I did it for myself? I became aware of one more thing: This is new to her. She has experienced moments of insights and intuition but never discovered her ability to see and sense both her own energies and that of her guides (the team, again) and the Divine forces. The contrast—the "Aha!"—in her new visions compared to her old way of seeing her world is bound to make an impression.

I'm not diminishing her experience—not at all. What she's seeing and sensing is powerful, colourful, and magical. I don't recall my first encounters with the depth of my soul and the "height" of my greater perspective being as spectacular as hers are, but I do remember how delightful it was to dive into and explore this world—my world—not to mention discovering I could do it. In fact, I've been doing it so "well," with more and more ease and clarity, it has become second nature. I can, in the flash of a moment, "see" or sense the energies of a situation, provided I choose to and am asked to do so. It's who I am now. It's who I was all along; I just didn't remember.

I got all this, but I wanted to reconnect with greater awareness and clarity to magic and higher wisdom. I engaged in one-on-one communications with my guides. I knew my team was with me, and I knew they were ready to listen the moment I connected. I had clogged up our "communication channels," though. It was time to clear them up. I decided to re-connect the way we used to practise when I did my training, the way I was showing my "student." I wanted to ask questions, tune in for the answers, and ask for help. I wanted to open and receive. For myself as well as for you, my dear reader. For anyone who would want to listen.

The word "allow" appeared to me as I googled "Gabriel," an archangel with whom I wanted to communicate. Usually,

I wouldn't google an energy—or angel—before connecting. I would meditate, tune in, and see what came, but I didn't quite trust myself. I remember little of what I read—I knew in my heart I didn't need that information. I needed that word, though: Allow. I sat down to meditate. I took a couple of deep breaths, "pulling myself together" and connecting to Source and the support of Mother Earth. I focused my intention and opened all my senses—physical and "supernatural." Then, when I was ready, I asked: "Gabriel, can you show yourself?"

I sat there, in focused stillness.

It took a little while, because as I've worked a great deal with helping and guiding other people, I'd almost forgotten to let myself receive. But as I leaned into "allowing," I felt a softening. A warmth. Something gentle kindling my heart and body.

I lost my concentration for a few minutes (I confess, my mind continues to play that trick on me at times—unless I work on other people. Which tells a story in itself, doesn't it?). Returning to my state of listening, I asked for a message. I asked Gabriel to show me what I needed to grasp in that moment.

The message I received was crystal clear: "Allow us to guide you. Lean into our guidance. Relax. Let us bring you all you need to find your way: the people, the opportunities, the ideas. We will bring it all. You've asked, and it's coming. Just relax. It's all you have to do."

And I knew it.

We've all heard this before, I suppose. Especially if you're in the business of manifesting, or trying to manifest. Ask. Trust. It shall come to you. Send the vibration out there and live as though it has already happened. Relax. Let the Universe bring it to you. Have you ever felt it? Or do you keep struggling and asking, "Why has it not materialised? Why is it taking so long? What am I doing wrong?", etc. When you discover it's up to you to manifest it, it's a short distance to blaming yourself for it not happening.

Well, stop. Right now. Sit down. Meditate. Ask a guide of your choosing: "What do I need to know right now?" (You don't need to know the guides' names. Ask "someone" to come forward. It's all it takes.) Then listen.

The answer might come like a nudge at the back of your mind, or in a flash. It can come as an image, a colour, a word, or a song. When you get a "message," let it seep into your body, mind, and soul. If you forget things, write it down. It's your life we're talking about. Your spirit. Your sense of self. Your Being. If nothing happens, try again. You'll get an answer.

It was exciting to connect with Gabriel again. I'm still floating on the experience. I'm allowing. For now, at least.

I'm writing this for your benefit (should you want it) but also so I can return to these pages and remind myself: Allow….

That's what I wanted to share today.

A lunch and a meditation later, still in my studio…

I have more on my mind. It took only a few minutes before I had to return to these pages. My encounter with Archangel Gabriel's energy inspired me deeply, and I invited in another archangel. (Whether you believe in angels doesn't matter. What I'm talking about is the energy we call "Gabriel." This time, there were two options: the one we call "Michael," and then "Raphael." I decided on Raphael—that was the energy, the "color" (a shade of green to my inner eye, which I understand as being Raphael) that showed up the strongest in the moment.

I sat in meditation, and "looked" with my mind's eye at this energy, wondering what the experience would bring. At first it felt shallow, but I stared it straight in the eye, so to speak (straight into its epicentre—into its heart). Again, I had an awareness of being told, "Allow the healing."

Now, "experts" in angels denote Raphael as the Great Healer, so this made sense to me. But the message of healing wasn't the interesting bit. It was the question that followed: *Why do you not allow the healing?*

So, I ask you: "Are you allowing the healing?"

If you're ill, emotionally or physically, and you're seeking help to heal (with traditional therapy or medicine, or otherwise), are you letting the healing come through? Or are you working hard trying to "fix" yourself by doing all the "right" things the therapist(s) tell you to do?

Allowing the healing has a distinct feeling. It's a soothing energy that lets you open your heart to receiving. "Receiving what?" you ask. Receiving Love. Love heals. It's as simple as that. I've said it before: All we need is Love.

I should advise you that all this energy stuff is subtle. Be kind and patient with yourself. It might take time to adjust your sensory system so you can feel these subtle differences—especially if your life is full of "noisy" things and you're not accustomed to embracing kindness. Give yourself some slack. In fact, let me guide you through a small exercise to see if you can sense it. Remember, be curious—always. Set the intention of exploring with wonder and amusement:

Meditation – Allow the Healing

Bring your awareness to an ailment or emotional pain you've been working to heal.

Now think of everything you've done—everything you've tried, every piece of advice you've followed, every effort you've made to heal. Acknowledge it all as part of your journey. Please (and this is important) do your best not to surrender to frustration or to judge yourself or your advisors for now. This is about observing the experiences so you can shift. Take a deep breath and accept the journey. Love yourself for all your efforts and remind yourself you are learning. You're searching, and with your search you are growing.

Now take another deep breath. As you exhale, feel all your old effort melting away or dissipating into the air. Repeat this a few times—until you can sense you're free from any judgement or emotions you've been holding on to.

When you're ready, take one more deep breath. Become aware of the moment: this is now. The past is gone.

Then you can search for the "allowing." Where in your experience is it? What does it feel like? Remember—it might be subtle in the beginning. It might escape your attention. You might almost have it, then lose the sensation again. Don't fret. Keep sensing, investigating—like with "the eye of the Divine." What does it mean to allow? How does it feel in your body, emotions, energy?

Play with these images. Imagine a beam of light from above flowing into your body through the top of your head. Imagine this light bathing your body, lingering in any part that's hurting. (If it's emotional, where does the emotion hide in your body—in your heart, mind, tummy? Anywhere else?). Imagine this light is Love (it is). Imagine receiving—truly receiving—this Love with all your being. Bathe in it. Allow it to fill you and expand beyond the outline of your body so you're engulfed in the light. Allow the light to give you what you need and receive, receive, receive. Allow.

Stay with this sensation as long as you want, and when you're ready, take a deep breath. Notice your surroundings and your body, and stretch.

Ah, one last thing. Whether or not you "got it," smile. You've just given yourself a beautiful moment of exploration. You've reminded your soul of your desire to heal and rise. Not to work or to try. To heal. You've shown your essence that you're willing to listen, that you're ready to learn and take your next step toward alignment and happiness. That deserves a smile.

Raphael's message made complete sense to me as it came through, and it stays with me. We can work as hard as we want to try to "fix" our ailments, but if we don't allow healing to happen, how can we heal? It would be like banging against a locked and barred steel door again and again. The door will never open unless someone lets it open. When they do, voilà! All you need to do is enter. With a smile, I might add….

I know these things might take time and patience "to get," but you'll never get it if you don't ask, or wonder. If you've tried the exercise above, you can experiment further:

Exercise – Allow the Healing

Practise leaning into the sensation of allowing for a moment. Remind yourself of the sensation. Try it again tomorrow. And the day after that. Try it a tad longer the following day. See where it takes you. I certainly will…

Have a gorgeous day, my friend. I must move on to my big project—this vision and dream of mine I've been working on for some time now. Remember? The one that caused me to abandon this manuscript for three years, and which has caused more than minor frustration at the time it's taking to materialise. I'll practise *allowing* this time around. I'll let the Universe bring me what I need to make it happen.

PART III

MASTER TRANSFORMATION

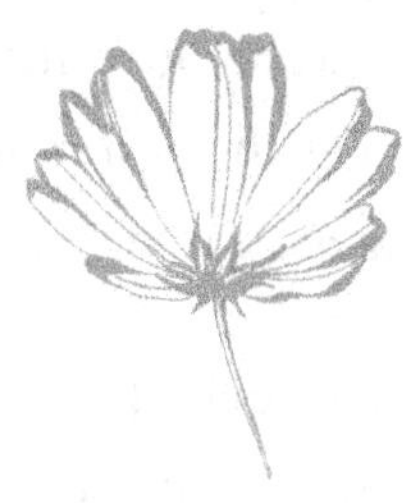

When I embarked on my journey, I found my path
covered with sticks and stones.
I was unable to find my way.
I began removing the obstacles,
gaining courage with every stick I brushed aside,
building strength with every stone I shifted.
I picked up the tools I found as I moved along.

Soon I could glimpse the
trail underneath the debris.
I stood up, lifted my gaze,
and felt the warming sun on my face.
I started walking, with curiosity, treading carefully at first,
moving the obstacles as they appeared with growing
confidence and ease.
I felt joy in my heart. Hope.
I could sense the outline of
my dream at the end of my trail.
It was no longer an unattainable mirage.

Then, suddenly, I stumbled.
A large rock blocked my path,
too big and heavy for me to shift.
It had been hidden under the sticks and stones.
I tried to walk around it,
but the surrounding forest was impenetrable.
I felt the shadows creeping in,
and lost sight of my vision.

Frightened and confused, I cried for help.
I prayed.

Then I shook my head in disbelief:
Had I learnt nothing?
Was I not bigger than my challenges after all?

I remembered the tools I had gathered.
I found the ones I needed and began
digging into the earth surrounding the rock.
My strength returned.
My courage.
The joy I had felt when
I first discovered my beautiful path.

The big stone started to shift,
and soon I could roll it out of my way.
I straightened my back, took a deep breath,
and smiled at the sun.
I had done it.
I had removed one of my biggest barriers,
one I hadn't been aware of,
one that had been hiding
deep in the soil for a long time.
I had remembered who
I was and conquered my fear.

I was ready to walk on once more.

My darling,

It's been nearly two weeks since I wrote last, and I'm going to be honest with you: I'm a healer and a seer, but no matter how many revelations I have, and no matter how connected I am, I'm still a human being. I sometimes stumble and fall and lose sight of my steps. It's part of life, regardless of how enlightened we've become. Sometimes we find ourselves in the dark. Why? There might be numerous reasons. If we ignore an old pattern or trauma too long, allowing it to accumulate while we're looking to the sky for answers and forgetting to attend to our human needs and experiences, the trauma will catch up with us. At times, it will confuse us until we can't hear our inner voice or divine guidance. We lose sight of our truth—our beauty, strength, freedom, and Love—and we grope around in the dark. We forget how our soul loves us and wants to show us the way so we can heal and rise, even if it means revealing to us that which is holding us back. In our confusion we might forget the gifts we've discovered in ourselves on our quest to rediscover who we are. We forget there's always a way out. We lose sight of our visions.

I know now that no matter how dark it may look, there's always a light there for us. No matter how aligned we might be, we're living a human experience, and there will be times when we stumble. When we experience fear, or we doubt everything we believe in, we needn't worry. We will prevail. Because regardless of how clouded our vision becomes, we are souls. Our souls never forget, and they never give up on us. Nor do our guides.

Tonight, my beloved, I'm writing to you from the centre of a massive transformation. It's been happening for a long time, of course, as I've opened to embrace my all. However, there are moments when the transformation feels like falling off a cliff, not like rising to a higher vibration. At these moments, I'm frightened. My whole life, and our life together, is undergoing a transition on so many levels, it's hard to keep an eye on the road ahead. Accepting and allowing seem vague concepts—there are too many changes at once. I'm doing my best to remain strong and supportive for you, my love, but within I'm trembling.

In every healing journey, we sometimes take one step forwards and ten steps back. Even though I've empowered myself over these past years, and grown in so many ways, I'm still vulnerable to insecurity and self-doubt. I still have to dig deep at times, and employ every tool I've gathered on my healing journey, to rise to the challenges placed before me. This is such a time.

When I woke up in the middle of the night, I couldn't remember who I am or why I'm here. I felt misplaced. Alone. Like I was "losing" everything: our home, my work, my money, my dreams, and, when you move to your dad's to be closer to your new school, you. (Though I try to hide it, I'm dreading the day you leave the "nest," especially because I don't know how you'll feel about my new home. Our new home. Will you enjoy coming there? Will we continue to have our gorgeous mornings together, and our evenings playing board games or watching our favourite TV series?)

It can be hard to keep the voices in our heads under control. I'm the first to admit that sometimes, no amount of breathing, meditation, or positive thinking will shut out the confused mind when it's running amok at 3:00 a.m. Last night, as I woke up, I felt my life spiralling downward. In my half-sleep, I thought, Can I manage life at all? *I questioned everything I've connected to in the last few years—everything I've shared with you here and taught people who have come to me for help.* "What do I know? I mean, really? What if it's all an illusion? What if it's all my imagination? Where's the truth?"

I looked out the window above my bed as if the cloud-free sky held the answers. I repeated these words in my mind (to whom I didn't know.): Talk to me, show me, guide me, talk to me, show me, guide me, talk to me, show me, guide me.

My body relaxed. I remembered I hadn't meditated for a while. I got out of bed, made a cup of tea, lit a candle, and sat down to meditate. Two words came to me: one tone.

I remembered how it all starts with that one tone. One word. One step. Yes, I'm still in the middle of a challenging transition, but I found my guidance again. I listened. I opened my Mac and wrote those two words: One tone.

⁓

One tone. That's where this all started, remember? One word. Then one sentence.

One tone got me started with my music. When you play one tone, it can go in any direction. As can a word. Or a step. When you play one tone and listen— truly listen— for the next tone, you'll hear the melody your soul is singing to you. You'll find the flow, and the music will unfold. You'll feel satisfied and at peace. When you create from curiosity and with a playfulness that comes from being in the moment, magic happens. Listen to the hints your inner guidance gives you. Your inner voice is the voice of your soul. It's a good voice, and it's connected to All That Is. To Love. To the one tone. It will take you to a good place.

My love, I won't deny it—sometimes I forget that tone and worry my music isn't good enough, complex enough, virtuoso enough, enough, enough. I forget to sit at the piano, take a breath, wait as I shift my focus to the moment, and start. With a tone. I forget to play because I want to play. But often—more often now than ever before—I remember. Then I play. Those moments always leave me elevated, with a satisfied heart and mind.

I'm sitting out on our lovely little terrace, surrounded by the sounds of nature in the night, and as I sit here, I realise I've forgotten to play that tone, to write that word, to take that one step that will move me towards my vision. My dream. I would say "purpose," but perhaps I'm living my purpose now, as I continue this search—this journey. Perhaps learning and navigating through the obstacles life provides, and discovering ways to be and love myself in the midst of the storm is what I'm here for?

I've written before that maybe there's no meaning to life. That doesn't help when you're frightened, of course. But there's the aspect I spoke of, finding the meaning in being true to ourselves and living in alignment—in joy. In Love. Of living in union with other souls who discover that same sense of alignment. There's the aspect of shifting your focus from the tip of your shoes and lifting your gaze to see the horizon. The sky. The miracles that surround us.

One tone. That's how music starts. It's all we need to move, to sing again, and to live, love, and be. Where will this tone, this one word, this one step take me? I don't know yet. I'll try to remember to listen and follow the music of my soul.

As I'm writing this, tears of relief are trickling down my cheek. I sense my heart softening, and I remember there's kindness in our world. I remember that we, magnificent beings that we are, are the messengers for this kindness. If only we remember to allow.

Much love and countless blessings to you, my dearest.
Thank you for being there.
Thank you for being you.

A thought later, still on our terrace…

Before I go back to bed, let me remind you (and myself) that however fearful or disconnected you may be, you can always ask for help. You can seek advice from friends or family, healing from professionals, and guidance from "above." (Ask, pray, cry out to the Universe, Source, God, or your "team." They're eager to guide you). You can open a book that appeals to you and read, do an exercise that will give you support, or sit with yourself and listen. Listen into and through your pain and distress until you feel the calm and hear your voice. The good voice.
Remember?

Today, I invite you to a place of stillness. Find a quiet place. Make yourself comfortable.

Meditation – Love Your Body

Take a deep breath. Bring your attention to this moment: the space you're in, the sensations in your body, and the emotions you hold in your heart. Pull yourself together. Any energy your emotions, fears, and dreams have sent into the past, or into the future, or to other people or other places: pull it in. (Use your hands in any way you like to do this.) Imagine you're gathering everything that is you in any form into your present moment and being, into your epicentre, your "knot," your body, and your heart.

Focus on your body. Reflect on how your body is part of you, and how it's doing its best to support you. No matter what your relationship with it in your day-to-day life is, and no matter what pain or illness you may have, for a moment, acknowledge your body as your friend—your "partner in crime." Bring your hands to different parts of your body: your head and face; your hands, fingers, feet, and toes; your back, hips, and buttocks. Give every part of you all the compassion and love you can—as if your body were your lover, your child, your closest ally. Your body is longing for your love. Your love will remind it of its strength and natural ability to heal. Love will give your body the energy it needs to continue supporting you. Embrace your body. Love it.

Talk to your body with kindness and words of gratitude. Even if you harbour patterns of self-loathing, self-rejection, or self-criticism—if you dislike your body or believe it to be failing you—try to rise above it. Come back to the embrace, the kindness. Trust your heart's ability to send love to every bit of your body.

Your heart doesn't discriminate. It doesn't judge. It loves. Allow it to do so.
In your mind's eye, step back a little. Let your heart do its work without interference. You don't have to control it. You can't control it. You can only feel it. If you can't feel your heart, don't worry. Just imagine. Your intention is enough. For now. Your soul—your subconscious—will get the message and help you remember. You don't need to believe it or understand it. You can open to the possibility that no matter how small or hidden it feels, no matter how distant, Love is at the core of your heart. Embrace the truth of this. Sink into the experience of it.

I have one more simple yet impactful healing meditation for you.

Meditation – Breathe Love

> Breathe into Love:
> Breathe in, "I am Love." Breathe out, "I love."
> Breathe in, "I am Love." Breathe out, "I love."
> Breathe in…. Breathe out….

Every person and soul that has ever sought my help, or who has sought to be "seen" from a higher perspective, has at some point shown me the Love in their heart. It's who we are. Can you feel it? If not, it may be that you've lived your life denying the love in your heart, so it's no wonder you can't feel it. You will. I'm sure of it. Not because I'm waving a magic wand right now (maybe I am?) so you'll "suddenly" get it, but because you're searching. You're a soul manifested in this world, searching for ways to reconnect and come closer to your truth. Any tool that comes your way is perfect for you at this moment—in your time. I'm writing from my heart, and my heartfelt wish for your highest good. It's a wish I share with your soul. We won't let you off the hook, either of us.

So, with the meditation above, all you must do is try. Hold the intention of exploring good things for yourself—including your body. If you can't experience those good emotions yet, think them. Imagine them. Say them. Start where you can. One word. One step. As you do, I promise wherever you are, and in whatever way you tune in, you're taking steps towards the delight of being in love, with your body, with yourself, with life, with people, with our world. With Creation.

As I sat down to read through the words I've written thus far, I realised my transition has taken me to a different place emotionally and spiritually than where I was when I started this book. I was already tapping into some amazing things back then, of course—many of which I've shared with you. But lately, I've spent more time tuning in and listening to the Divine wisdom within me. Not always, but enough that now, whenever I choose and whenever I remember to do so, I can connect my awareness and physical being to my higher knowing and wisdom, my "higher self." I lean—or step—into her, feeling her vibration and handing all my questions and confusion to her. She's always there—ready to hold me. Around me, within me, above me, and below me, she's in touch with the past, present, and future. Pure, patient, understanding, loving, and strong, she masters the art of resting (not my best human quality). She knows how to rise and how to heal. She knows how to *be*.

How did I get here?
By wondering. By investigating.

By meditating, yes, though not always by sitting in silence with my eyes closed. As I've told you before, I can just as easily meditate on the move—walking, swimming in the sea, cleaning, showering—in the sense that I can tune in and stay present in the moment and with the wisdom I'm seeking. Like when I tried to find the "eye of the Divine," remember? I meditate because I choose to sit with myself and listen. Or take myself for a walk and seek. I don't always "hear" anything, but I wonder. And investigate. And discover. It's exciting and rejuvenating. It's Home.

Let me tell you this: There's no place like home. Being present with my entire self in the moment—any moment—is Home. I experience my essence not only with my "imagination" but also almost physically, as a vibration, a caress, on my skin, my body, when I lean into it (I do! You should try it—explore it). It's Home.

I know who I am now. I get how I'm connected to the Divine, to the Earth, to other people. At least more or less. When I lose sight of Home (again, we all do), I trust my soul will guide me through it. If I'm desperate and painful emotions overwhelm me, I shout out to the sky, crying for help, relief, and guidance. I always come out of it. I always return to my newfound reality—

my Home. It might take time, but my foundation is solid, and my heart—my soul's anchor, my "knot"—is ready to soften and love once more. I know I'll find my way because since I began my awakening journey, each time I stumbled into darkness, I reconnected to my essence.

A few years ago, I experienced a deep crisis. I discovered the reality I'd been living was based on lies. Not only lies people I cared for told—but also lies I'd told myself about myself. I'd been pretending I was happy without recognising what happiness felt like. I'd denied my worthiness and desire to experience joy. My whole life seemed to come apart (it was a blessing, as I would see later). Reality struck me: it's all a lie. Everything. Even the beautiful revelations that had shown me there's more to life than meets the eye, and that we, in essence, are Love, seemed false. It was as if a heavy curtain covered my vision, and I discovered *I could stay in the belief that this is it.* The way my dad did: *This is life: We struggle, we do our chores, we move forward to make our lives work to the best of our ability in our societal structures, and that's it.* Why on earth should I consider anything else? I got it. I understood—nay, I felt it in my entire being—how my father had experienced that what he saw and perceived to be the truth in his physical reality was all there was. I understood where he'd come from and almost convinced myself he'd been right. I kept thinking: *All those people who talk about the higher self, the Universe, the Law of Attraction, inner peace, being connected—in short, everything I've learnt these last years—must be wrong. They're phoneys. I'm a phoney.* Until I regained my sense of self.

The last time I experienced intense fear—remember? I awoke in the night and was shaken by the changes happening in my life. Goodness, it was just a week ago… The last time I felt this, I remembered that experience in my past, and nearly let myself go there again. For a few moments. Until I sat down and meditated.

What I didn't mention earlier was that the next morning I had to conduct a course on reconnecting to unconditional, Divine Love. I was nervous. Although I'd meditated in the night and restored my sense of self, I still wasn't at peace. Did I have anything to contribute? My doubt threatened to bring me down once more. My old fears crept in again—fears of not being good enough, of being a fraud, and of disappointing my course participants—people who had paid a fair amount of money to receive my guidance.

Another meditation, with another cry for help. I received the healing energy of something or someone "out there," and again experienced a moment of peace. The fear dissipated, and I felt relief. I felt warmth in my heart, softness, strength, and subtle, gentle, kind love. Then I recognised the message I had received once before: "Allow the healing."

I could meet my lovely clients and lead them to their own connection to Love. My essence, my higher self, my guides, the Divine—whatever it was—had reminded me of who I am. I could choose to remember.

It took a little while to regain my natural state of curiosity, excitement, peace, and love, as sometimes happens when you encounter fear (especially if the "noise" of life gets in the way). This time, my energy went into preparing the house for sale. I did it. We sold the house, and we can look forward to a new chapter—whatever it may bring. We can enjoy some restful time in the garden and on our little beach before we pack and prepare to move. It will allow me to restore my energy and regain my balance. I feel connected to my light again as I write this, and I'll do my best to keep the flow through any obstacles that might come my way. Am I nervous about what's coming? Yes. A little. All will be different, and I'm leaving a beautiful community of friends behind. I'll embrace myself on the journey. I'll return to my foundation and connect to the greater wisdom as much as I can. If I forget, I'll try to be kind to myself. I'll ask for help as often as I can.

I feel vulnerable, as we often do when facing big changes, but I'm strong. Let the waves wash over me. Maybe their force will overwhelm me for a minute. I might even stumble. But I choose to live in alignment with all that I am. I choose to return Home as often as I can. I know it to be good and true for me as a soul, a human being, a woman, and a mother.

As I continue healing, the light of my essence brightens and is reflected in the radiant summer sun. My joy of writing returns. As does my longing to create music and build my vision of a healing centre for the children and the young. I want to meditate. Swim in the ocean. Celebrate with my beloved friends. Relax. Be.

Fredrik, my love,
*   Here's to life.*
*   Here's to our journey forward, together and apart.*
*   You'll be living in a different city, but I won't be*
far away.
*   If you need me, I'm here for you. Always. You know that.*
*   I'm proud of you. I think you know that, too.*
*   So here's to you.*
*   And me.*
*   And all that we are.*

Meditation – Reconnect to Your Essence

When you find yourself in a place of confusion and distress, stop.

Simply choose to stop for a moment.

Find a quiet corner—in the bathroom, in your bedroom, in the forest, by the sea—and sit or stand quietly.

Close your eyes.

Breathe. Imagine gathering your energy—all of you—into your body and heart.

Breathe again. Imagine stepping onto your foundation—onto a circle of light on the ground, or onto a raised platform.

Sense yourself connecting to this foundation, stretching roots of energy down into it.

Bring your attention to your heart. Ask:
    "What do I need to know right now?"
    "What does my soul want to tell me?"
    "How can I navigate in the best possible way through
this situation?"

Wait.

Repeat the questions if you need to.

Listen.

Breathe.

Observe what happens to your body.

Don't worry if you don't get a "clear" answer—one you
can understand with your mind.

Observe. Allow. Let your essence, your heart, do what
it wants to do.

Let your soul help you.

Do this as often as you need to until you recognise your
beauty again. Your wisdom. Your strength.

Until you remember who you are, and trust that you
have yourself no matter what.

You'll have yourself at every moment on your journey.

You can never lose your soul. Your essence.

It is You.

Soon, my dear reader, it will be time to leave you. I've shared what I can for the moment. I trust there's a message in here that will move you, inspire you, touch your heart, and give you hope and courage to remember who you are. I cannot say it enough: You are Love.

You are Love in and of yourself, because you are. There's no mystery, no condition, no hidden secret. Only that. What a wonderful world this would be if we all embraced the Love we hold in our beings. Until we're ready to do so fully, every moment we spend in contentment and delight (by choosing that which gives us joy) will reunite us with this Love.

Again, if you can't remember what joy is, recall what once brought bliss into your life. Yes, use your mind, that magnificent tool. Use your memory to bring those uplifting experiences back into your life. Try it out (in secret if you must) but give yourself the opportunity to rediscover joy. Give yourself the gift of reconnecting to your unique essence, your truth.

Recently, my higher guides shared an interesting perspective. It reminded me of the experience I wrote about earlier, when I realised I should stop "trying" to play the piano and focus in on the tones instead. If you find yourself stuck in limbo or in the dark, if it frustrates you that life is not going your way and you find yourself unable to make your dreams and wishes come true, don't try to make it happen. Let go. You've stated your wish. That's enough. Now, go out and do what gives you joy. Walk in the forest, swim in the sea, meet a friend, make love, or eat an ice cream (with joy). Stop the voice that's telling you it's not good for you. There's nothing so good for you as that which gives you joy. (It's been proven scientifically, I think.) Play with your child, read a book, watch a feel-good film, listen to music, or drink a cup of hot chocolate (stop that voice). You name it. Do it.

You wonder, "Why would this help?" It puts you in a state of alignment with yourself and with your superpowers as an unlimited being in a body. Your eyes and ears will receive any sign or clue that's in tune with what you wish to do. Or create. Or have. As you enter a café, or head for the beach, you could meet the person who can guide you to your next step. You might not, of course, but you might. Who knows? Get out there. Vibrate at that lovely frequency of joy and love while spreading that infectious smile of yours around. Joyous smiles are always infectious, didn't you realise? Joy's vibration ignites the spark in our heart and opens up our vision, our intuition, and our connection to higher wisdom—within ourselves and beyond. It's a wonderful, playful superpower. The prospect of bringing it into our lives should excite us. Are you excited? Why not?

"Do I need to stay in joy all the time?" you ask. Of course not. Give that idea up right away. We're here to break through the dense limitations of the physical realm and bring it up to par with the beautiful Love that we are. We must break through the barriers, stories, and belief systems that have shaped our reality so we can make sense (as senseless as the reality might look sometimes) of our lives here on earth. This is our opportunity to use our delicious superpowers to love ourselves into a better state and love the world into a better place.

There's hope for our world. We can achieve peace. Balance. We can create a kind world where the essence of Love will guide us every day, everywhere, every step of the way. This is possible because there are so many of us seeking to rise. For each human being who dares to open up and reconnect, there are more human beings touched by others' joy, compassion, and love, and they too will recognise the spark in their soul which is waiting for them to let it shine. Then, when the "100th ape" has reignited the spark, we all will. We can all shine our light once more.

Dearest Fredrik,

It's time to share a glimpse of the big vision I mentioned, the vision that appeared as I saw the ad for the lottery. Do you remember? I was looking at a chateau in France that was for sale. As you know, I didn't win the lottery— not then, and not at any other time I've bought a ticket. I did something far more valuable, far more interesting and challenging. I developed a sketch for my vision: a vision that holds the seed of peace, balance, and the well-being of your generation, the generation that will take our world to a new, more peaceful future. The dream holds magic, love, collaboration, empowerment, self-worth, and self-expression as its guiding lights.

I've shared parts of my dream with you before, my love, but let me take you further into the vision.

Imagine visiting a chateau in Southern France. Imagine driving up a long driveway lined with tall, green trees. There's a bend in the road, and as you turn the bend, you see the building—its beauty and serenity. It's surrounded by an abundant garden, rich in colourful flowers and trees. You see a pool in between the branches. There's a field with horses in it, and beyond, a forest. You step out of the car, and you hear music. A choir. You follow the sound and arrive at a round pavilion amongst the trees. Twenty to thirty children are rehearsing with a group of musicians. Their song is unfamiliar to you in its rhythm and harmonies, as if it's from a land far away, yet it's easy to absorb. You sit down and listen, captivated by the energy and the happy faces, all focused on the conductor. When the music has finished, you approach the conductor and ask, "What is this all about?"

"We're preparing for a grand festival," she tells you. "A festival for the celebration of life. Children of all ages and multiple nationalities have worked through the year towards this goal, in collaboration with professional musicians and artists, and they're thrilled. My team and I have collaborated with parents, carers, and teachers in guiding the children to discover their worth and passion, empowering them to find their unique expression— through music, art, nature, and play. In our world," she says, "we've forgotten that play is the only job children need to have. Through play they grow, learn, and create. It's the guiding principle of our work here, and we bring it into our work with the adults, too. Not just the children's carers, but anyone seeking to contribute to peace in our world. We believe that through our work with the young, we can contribute to a better world, that the children will create a better world for themselves if they're given the opportunity to be who they are at their core, with all their dreams, qualities, and passion. That's why this place is special. It's the children. Not the building." She looks at you eagerly, and you see a twinkle in her eyes. "Although, I'll admit the beauty of the chateau and its surroundings helps, of course. It makes it possible for us to invite VIPs to come here and work and heal, too. That's how we get the funds for our work with the children."

Yes, my vision is a chateau—a physical centre from which a restorative and empowering vibration can radiate out to the world and ignite a spark in young people who do not yet embrace their worth or their power. I aim to gather these young people into a joyful, safe, and peaceful community where kindness and respect prevail. I want to give them a microphone so everyone can hear them and understand the wisdom they hold in their hearts. Just as you do, my love.

Then I'll bring adults in to listen. The leaders. The decision makers. The teachers. I wish to show them the gifts that your generation—gifts as old as Creation itself, however young in body you may be—brings to our world.

You possess gifts we cannot afford to ignore, and you're just as connected to your light as anyone else. Maybe more. You've had less time to clog it up with misconstrued beliefs and patterns. Most of you also come to this world with a strong intention to lift our gaze and help us rise. You've come in confusing times, though, with fear and stories of destruction dominating the information presented to you—be it in school, on TV, in films, on social media, or through frightened parents. I intend to remind your peers of what joy is, so they too can honour their right to shine and experience happiness, love, and peace. Just like you and I will. I hope they remember who they are, and the beauty they hold in themselves. Like you. And me.

Am I there yet? No. Not in physical form. But the vision is there and the energies are lining up to make the dream a reality. The woman in the tale above might be me, or it might be one of my future colleagues. Whatever the case, when I listen, I can hear the sounds of the children and feel the thrill of gathering like-minded people in that stunning place. I envision a worldwide online community formed around the chateau, all with the aim of creating a better world. It's bound to happen, because I see—from watching you grow and rise to embrace your potential—the wisdom and light you and your peers bring with you. If you stop to listen beyond the noise of the world that surrounds you, you can imagine a world in which everyone knows their worth, and a world where everyone is kind—to others and to themselves.

Imagine the peace we would have.
The excitement.
The joy.

Have I told you how much I love you? Yes? Well, it won't harm you to be reminded of it from time to time. I'm your mother, after all...

EPILOGUE

So, my beloved,

Here we are. A new chapter has begun. You've moved to the city to live with your dad, and you've started a new school. I've moved to my childhood home—not too far from you. I've made this new home into a cosy little den, and I'm pleased you enjoy spending time here. Our lovely mornings and lazy evenings together continue.

Has it been an easy move? No. As with any big shift, this one has brought its challenges, for both of us. Everything is different for you. You've had to adjust your way of living and organizing your days, and you've had to take on more responsibility. I've faced disruptions and confusion as old patterns and stories from my childhood have come back to haunt me. We've parted with dear friends, and sometimes I've felt lost and sad at having to leave our old life behind.

But we have each other, and we have an unexplored path ahead of us—parts of which we'll tread together, and parts apart. As we should. I'll always be your mother, and I'll always love you, but you're getting ready to embark on your own, independent journey. That journey will be yours to explore. Not mine. I'll witness it with affection, and I'll offer my guidance when you ask for it, but I can never take part in it unless you want me to.

It's interesting to consider my role as a mother in light of the lessons I've learnt these past years. Especially now, as the time to send you off onto your own path is approaching. I see and understand that although we're all connected, none of us can "own" another human being—or their soul. We can love, play, and dance together, but each human being plays their part in the Whole. Like a piece in a puzzle, we fit into the world exactly where we should with our colours and shape. Our timbre. We can never take the place of another piece—another human being. We can never force another person to fit into a slot that isn't theirs. Not without pain and conflict. We can only do our best to discover our own shape and find our place in the greater picture. We can, however, marvel and rejoice at the colourful images that emerge as each individual finds their place, one by one. That's when the flow emerges. That's when we find peace.

No matter where you go or what you choose to do in your life, the steps are yours to take. The choices are yours to make. I realise you find making decisions challenging at times. I've seen you battle with yourself as your mind sets a trap for you, telling you to do "the right thing." Just remember this: there is nothing—nothing—more "right" than that which comes from your heart. Your heart—a beautiful channel for your soul—holds the truth. Your truth. If you choose from this truth (from that which gives you joy) unapologetically, you'll do well. Joy is the only compass you need. It will help you make those decisions with ease and grace as you honour who you are and fill your life with those gorgeous emotions that are your nature. That's when you live your life from Love. All I can do is love you. Support you. Share thoughts with you. Reflect with you on your choices when you ask me to. Welcome you when you seek rest in my embrace—if you feel I'm the one who can provide the rest you're looking for. As any parent would, I'll have to work to remember to step back and let you come in your own time. I'll do my best. If I forget, please show me. I'll receive the reminder gratefully.

So, my dearest, you must choose for yourself what to fill your journey with. Will you nourish the little flowers along the path, tend to the large trees that give you shade in the heat, or climb to the top of a mountain to see the world? Only you can decide. I will, however, ask that you listen to the vibration of your heart. Let your curiosity guide you. Look around. Explore. Seek the answers to your questions, and open your arms to the people who invite you to be you. Walk away from those who want to stop you or act with ill intent towards you. Forgive them—they've not yet discovered who they are. Smile and love not only yourself and your loved ones but All That Is. Unconditionally. Marvel at the magic and beauty of your world. Look at the stars from time to time and make a wish. Bathe in the moon's light. Let the sun warm you. And when you feel alone, let those who instil a sense of calm and peace in you hold you. Let them love you until you're ready to embrace yourself. Allowing and receiving love—unconditional, free love—is an act of love for yourself, and for Creation. It's the most healing gift you can give yourself and your people. Your world.

Should old stories come back to haunt you, remember, when you're on the path to heal and rise, your soul will bring forward that which you must release. It will guide you to alignment and strength, so you can come forever closer to Home. Peace. It's your unique opportunity to heal, but don't worry. If you're not ready to grasp it the first time, or the second, your soul will keep bringing the patterns before you until you're able to face them and shift. As I've said before, your soul will not give up on you.

When I landed in my childhood home after our move, my old stories and trauma came to the surface. They seemed unbearable at one point... until I remembered that this is my opportunity to heal and to reconnect to who I am. It's the moment I can shake off that which I've not yet released. I can strengthen my foundation so I can see my passion, hear my inner voice more clearly, and become more myself. Then I can embrace myself and move on to a life my heart chooses.

Sometimes I sense the messages of my soul—the part of me that knows what I need and can create—like a distant whisper. It's as if there's a thin veil that obscures those messages, until I've acknowledged, accepted, and released all the limiting thoughts that created the veil. Then I'm able to see my truth. Just as I did with the eye of the Divine. Once I've discovered it, I can return to that truth and repeat it until it becomes my new default—my "knowing." That's when new doors open, and I can recognise the opportunities that invariably come my way. Why invariably? For the same reason emotions can heal and nothing will ever stay the same: everything moves. Because everything is energy. There's a great liberation in remembering that.

All the work you do to come closer to yourself works. I experienced that too, after our move. I received an invitation to a class reunion of the people I went to elementary school with. My time at that school wasn't happy. My classmates excluded and rejected me, and other kids bullied me. The last time I went to a class reunion, I still navigated my life with fear as my default. I remember thinking I had to prove myself at that gathering, and became self-absorbed in my struggle to say and do the "right" things and show them I had "become something," that I had risen from the shy, timid, clumsy girl I had felt I was back then. I can't remember the other people at that reunion—I remember only my narrow view.

This time, however, I knew who I was. I felt strong, empowered, beautiful, and at ease with myself and the people who were there. I'd been looking forward to meeting them and learning more about who they were and what life had offered them. After a round of "What has this class meant to you and your life, and what do you remember?" (I mentioned a few precious memories—there were a few of those too), a woman apologised to me for the way she had treated me at school. I noticed that the emotions from those days weren't part of me anymore. They had evaporated. I felt only peace and contentment, and compassion for my fellow classmates. I told her from my heart that all was well, there was nothing to forgive, and she shouldn't spend a moment longer worrying about it. My quest to release and heal my old stories had rewarded me.

So you see, my dearest Fredrik, allowing yourself to rediscover your truth—your essence—has its benefits. More than that, I believe doing so is your sole responsibility as an eternal soul in a body, because it allows you to live authentically and from Love. It allows you to share your beauty and magnificence with other people—other souls. And who knows? You might be the shining example that ignites a spark in other people, so they too find the courage to embark on a discovery towards their truth.

No matter what way you choose to express yourself, whatever you do from a place of amusement and delight will let you be a beacon of light. You've chosen to study music. For now. Music is one of the most powerful mediums for shining your light that I can imagine. It's pure vibration, and it's global. It's healing and enlightening if you don't lose yourself to ideas of "doing it right," or "having to be better," but instead, you play and create from joy. Trust me, I know the difference. Playing from excitement, curiosity, and exploration—rather than from "trying" or "doing"—allows you to share your heart gracefully and with ease. It allows you to touch people's souls. Your music might become a healing experience for both you and your audience as your pure, healing vibration flows into the world through the tones you play. There's no right or wrong. There's only Love. In the moment. It's all you have to remember. Remember it well.

So here's to you and your future, Fredrik. Here's to your peers and the power you all carry with you into our world.

I trust you'll use it to the best of your ability. I trust you'll make this world a better place for yourselves.

And here's to all the parents out there who are searching for their truth so they can be stronger, more authentic guides for their children. Let's not worry about being "perfect" in the eyes of someone else. Let's be a perfect example of us. Let's be ourselves. That's more than enough.

Thank you for listening to my story. I hope you found what you were looking for. Keep searching so you'll find the answers. Then, when you're tired of the search, relax. Rest. Play. Have fun. Without enjoyment—what would it all be for?

I wish you a beautiful adventure.

All my love,
Mum.

Acknowledgements

A multitude of people have contributed to this book by being part of my journey—whether through their teachings, their support and love, or by providing me with the challenges that have taught me what I needed to learn to grow and heal. I thank each one of you. I could not have taken this journey without every single turn, road bump, and hill—whether I brought them upon myself, or you provided me with them, and I couldn't have written this book without having been on the journey. Still, there are people who have participated in creating and completing this book.

First, I'd like to thank my wonderful editor, Michael Ireland. Your expertise, respect for my voice, and warm and encouraging guidance has been invaluable, and you've taught me more about writing a book than I imagined there was to know.

The beautiful ladies at PRESStinely—Kristen Wise and Maíra Pedreira—have guided me through the process of self-publishing and of bringing the book out to an audience in the most beautiful, professional, and generous way. Thank you for being there and sharing your impressive knowledge, enthusiasm, warmth, and creativity with me.

Patrick Chassagne—I owe you a big Thank You for helping me find my way in creating and building my business and vision. You haven't given up on me despite my many shifts and turns, and you keep offering your wisdom and sound, grounded advice. You're the "mystery person" who prompted me to write this book. It might not have materialised without your perceptive encouragement.

Ann-Karin, thank you for shining your light and showing me who I am. Although we've gone separate ways, your guidance and wisdom stays with me. I am eternally grateful.

There are numerous healers and "seers" out there who bring their gifts with integrity, love, and humility—and more are rising. I applaud every one of you for following your heart and guidance and for bringing your light to our world. Some of you have been important contributors to my journey:

To all my intuitive, "spiritual" teachers and guides—thank you for showing me how to find my path towards empowerment, growth, and enlightenment. You've all played a big part in my discovery of the magic and Love that was waiting for me to reconnect to it: Princess Märtha Louise and Elisabeth Nordeng of Astarte/Soulspring—you opened the door to this journey for me. I'll never forget the interview we did before enrolment, where you told me "You know this—you just have to remember." I felt "seen." My whole body tingled with excitement, and there was no doubt in my heart that I would join your course if you would have me. Happily, you did. Your brilliant, highly intuitive, and compassionate teachers and healers Louise Wilhelmine Lund and Katja Marty Bye were the most beautiful guides I could have dreamt of. Thank you!

Anett Powell Wang of Thetakoden was my next step in opening and enhancing my intuitive healing powers. You showed me how to explore my inner vision and higher perspective with curiosity and humour, and you helped me later when I felt stuck and alone in my continued search. You also offered your beautiful guidance and healing to Fredrik's father after his illness. Your work has been a gift to us all—I thank you.

To Ulla Suokko, thank you for your wise guidance and reminder to "Stop playing the piano if it makes you heavy. Only play when your heart tells you to do so," and for giving me the perspective of "the eye of the Divine." It's been one of the most transformative lessons of my life.

A big thanks to all the wonderful coaches who offer their wisdom online and in print, allowing those who seek guidance to receive it no matter where they are. Some of your courses have made (and continue to make) a great impact on my forever-growing awareness and comprehension of the beauty that I, and all of us, carry within. To Anita Moorjani, Mike Dooley, Christie Marie Sheldon, Tony Robbins, Marije Terloin, Jeffrey Allen, Burt Goldman, Regan Hillyer, Florencia Andrés, Gerard Adams, Ken Honda, and Vishen Lakhiani, thank you. Your work is priceless, and you're helping countless people connect to their potential and essence.

A handful of impactful healers and coaches have provided me with empowering and loving guidance and healing along the way. I thank you for being there and bringing forward your clarity, light, and compassion. Your guidance has been invaluable and has shown me how I can continue my expansion, growth, and "homecoming." To Mari Manzetti, Monica Evaldsdatter Dahlskjær, Gretha Dimmen, Hilde Aga Brun, Eva Moldova, Live Storruste at Klinikk 10a, and the readers at MicheleKnight. com, thank you from the bottom of my heart.

Bente and Hildegunn C, I'm grateful for the fourteen years we had together as a performing group. In spite of my stage fright and fear, we had a multitude of fantastic experiences, both on- and off-stage. Our journey together was one of growth and discovery, and I wouldn't have been here without those experiences. Thank you.

To all my clients: thank you for trusting me with your heart and soul, and for allowing me to "see" you and guide you to come closer to your truth. To Love. Every session we've had has taught me something unique. You all have a special place in the world, and I honour you for your search to uncover your full potential. Never give up!

It took a while before I shared with anyone in my life that I was writing a book. I wanted to hold the process close to my heart and see where it would go before sharing. However, I have some beautiful friends, old and new, who have supported me in everything I do and dream of—including this book once I revealed the "secret." I value these friendships and acknowledge and cherish your love and support. Thank you for walking by my side through the storms and for joining me in laughter and all life's beautiful moments. Thank you for letting me be me:

Astrid, Camilla, Anette, Einar, Susanne, Vidar, Line, Christine, Hildegunn S, Gulli, Ekua, Maria, and Therese.

And then my family—for whom I will always be grateful. You've shown me the way through your guidance, but also through our differences. Thank you to…

My dad for playing the piano while I was sleeping below, and for keeping the twinkle in your eyes despite all your pain and strife. Your life was not an easy one, and we all felt it, but I hold the memory of your essence in my heart always. You're free now—I feel you. You were a guiding light when I was little, and you're a guiding light again, now that you have released your pain and freed your spirit once more.

My mum for always being there, supporting me through life, and doing all you could—and can—to keep me safe. You've shown me how to welcome people of all kinds, cultures, and philosophies into my life, recognising their warmth and welcoming their differences. You've travelled the world several times and have brought the world back home—expanding my horizon and allowing me to keep my gaze on the wider perspective. You planted the seed of tolerance for people of all kinds, and it became my guiding principle later in life.

Pål—my cool, funny, creative, and talented brother, who is always there for me. I have no doubt you would travel the world for me if I needed you to. I hope you realise I would do the same for you. I'm your biggest fan: I love spending time with you, and I love how you've embraced and supported Fredrik from the day he was born. Though younger than me, you still stood up for me when you heard someone bully me—as you do with anyone you see being treated unfairly. Your values are sound and beautiful, and I couldn't have wished for a better role model for Fredrik. I love your family, too— Gemma, Spike, and Buddy—and am grateful for the bond we've created together. Always.

Nicolay—you've given me some of the greatest challenges of my life. I wouldn't have been here without them. They were the famed "blessings in disguise." I'm sorry for your illness—I've grieved it. Yet it brought us closer to each other so that today we can share a friendship I didn't think possible (although my intuition tried to tell me). I knew the first time I met you that something was bound to happen between us. I didn't know it was the most beautiful gift in the world: our beloved son. Thank you.

Alva and Rebekka—my beautiful "bonus" daughters. Thank you for welcoming Fredrik and me into your lives with such grace. It was abrupt, but you opened your arms to us, took Fredrik into your hearts, and allowed me to embrace and love you. You're both strong, talented, and gorgeous. Hold on to yourselves through any trials and keep searching for your hearts. You will both rise—I know you will. I'm proud of you both.

And Fredrik. My love. Thank you for coming into my life. Thank you for showing me the way by offering your light to my world. Thank you for being you. You inspire me, challenge me, and teach me lessons all the time—merely by being who you are. This book says enough, I think. I can only repeat: I love you. Always.

Emma

Bibliography

Books:

Anderson, Suzanne. *The Way of the Mysterial Woman: Upgrading How You Live, Love, and Lead.* Berkeley: She Writes Press, 2016.

Braden, Gregg. *Secrets of the Lost Mode of Prayer.* London: Hay House UK Ltd., 2006.

Dooley, Mike. *Leveraging the Universe and Engaging the Magic.* New York: Atria Books, 2011.

Elworthy, Scilla. *Pioneering the Possible.* Berkely, CA: North Atlantic Books, 2014.

---. *Business Plan for Peace.* London, UK: Peace Direct, 2018.

Sanders, Candia. *Soul Rays: Discover the Vibratory Frequency of Your Soul.* Carlsbad, CA: Balboa Press, 2013.

Stibal, Vianna. *ThetaHealing: Introducing an Extraordinary Healing Modality.* Carlsbad, CA: Hay House Inc., 2011.

Suokko, Ulla. *Signs of the Universe.* nc: Ulla Suokko/ WiseWoman, 2020.

Tolle, Eckhart. *The Power of Now: A Guide to Spiritual Enlightenment.* Novato, CA: New World Library, 1999.

Watson, Lyall. *Lifetide: A Biology of the Unconscious*. London, UK: Hodder and Stoughton, 1979.

Media and Online References:

Lennon, John, and McCartney, Paul. "All You Need Is Love." The Beatles. George Martin, Producer. *Magical Mystery Tour*. Recorded Olympic Sound Studios, Barnes, London, 1967.

New York Post. "Students insult plants in unique anti-bullying experiment." May 8, 2018. https://nypost.com/2018/05/08/students-insult-plants-in-unique-anti-bullying-experiment/ (Accessed April 2, 2024).

Roddenberry, Gene. *Star Trek*. Norway Productions/Desilu Productions/Paramount Television, Los Angeles, CA, 1966 – 1969.

Wikipedia. "Hundredth Monkey Effect." https://en.wikipedia.org/wiki/Hundredth_monkey_effect (Accessed June 8, 2023).

Courses:

Lund, Steffi. *Klassisk Yoga*. Nesodden, Norway, 2013 – 2014.

Powell Wang, Anett. «ThetaHealing®: Basic DNA & Dig Deeper». *Thetakoden*. Lørenskog, Norway, 2017 – 2018.

Princess Märtha Louise and Elisabeth Nordeng. Intuitive Reading & Healing. Astarte Inspiration (later Soulspring). Oslo, Norway, 2012 – 2015.

Online Courses:

(All URLs accessed February 15, 2024)

Allen, Jeffrey. Cultivating Intuition & A Balanced Mind. https://

www.mindvalley.com/trainers/jeffrey-allen.

Andres, Florencia. The Champion Mindset. https://www.mindvalley.com/champion.

Goldman, Burt. Quantum Jumping. Mindvalley. https://www.mindvalley.com/quantum.

Hillyer, Regan. The Art of Manifesting. https://www.mindvalley.com/manifesting.

Honda, Ken. Money EQ. Mindvalley. https://www.mindvalley.com/money.

Moorjani, Anita. Discover the Transformative Power of Near-Death Experiences. https://theshiftnetwork.com/NearDeathExperiences?&utm_medium=affiliate&utm_source=infusionsoft.

Powell Wang, Anett. ThetaKoden, Mindflow Mastery for Livsendring. https://www.thetakoden.no (Also in-person courses).

Sheldon, Christie Marie. Unlimited Abundance. https://www.mindvalley.com/abundance.

Terluin, Marije and Mike Dooley. Past Life Regression. https://club.tut.com/past-lives-online

About the Author

Emma Rowena is a musician, performer, intuitive reader, healer, meditation guide, and emerging social entrepreneur, helping people find peace, purpose, and healing in their lives. Emma was born in the UK, grew up in Norway, and has lived in Cuba and the USA. With her bilingual and bicultural heritage, Emma never felt at home in one place. She always felt more part of the greater world, and the years abroad helped her connect to her energy and colours. Inspired by her music-loving, piano-playing father, Emma studied to be a classical pianist. For nearly two decades, she made her living teaching children to play the piano and performing with some of Norway's most renowned singers and soloists.

Motherhood became a transformative journey for Emma, leading her to embrace her healing and personal growth. She is now a certified intuitive reader, healer, and ThetaHealing® practitioner. Combining her love for music with a passion for the well-being of the younger generation, Emma envisions creating a healing centre for children and youth, enabling them to discover their unique expression and developing solutions for a better, more sustainable and compassionate world. She shares her insights in this, her first book. Emma engages with her audience both online and in person, meditates, cooks, and finds solace in nature with her dog, always seeking the next step in her journey of helping, healing, and creating a better life.

www.emmarowena.no

audience both online and in person, meditates, cooks, and finds solace in nature with her dog, always seeking the next step in her journey of helping, healing, and creating a better life.

Dear Beloved Readers,

As you turn the final page of *You. Me. And All That We Are: Unveiling Your Life's Beauty and Magic – A Mother's Heartfelt Testimony to Her Son*, I hope the journey within these pages has touched your heart and soul.

To continue nurturing the seeds of inspiration I have planted in this book, I invite you to explore further resources on my website: https://www.emmarowena.no/. Here, you'll discover downloadable PDF exercises and extended meditation audio recordings to deepen your connection with the insights shared in these chapters.

Stay connected and be part of my community by subscribing to my newsletter. Receive timely updates on upcoming events, exclusive services, and more. Your journey doesn't end here. It's an ongoing exploration of the beauty and magic life has to offer.

For daily doses of inspiration and guidance, follow me on social media:

- Facebook: https://www.facebook.com/emmarowenahansen/
- Instagram: https://www.instagram.com/emmarowena/
- LinkedIn: https://www.linkedin.com/in/emma-rowena-hansen/
- YouTube: https://www.youtube.com/@emmarowena6136

Thank you for being a part of this transformative experience. May you fill your days with love, joy, and the magic that resides within you.

With gratitude, Emma Rowena

www.ingramcontent.com/pod-product-compliance
Lightning Source LLC
LaVergne TN
LVHW010331200726
843507LV00010B/1438